Praise for
Demystifying IT

"In this book, you will find an application of practical and pragmatic thinking that removes the shroud of mystery from IT. Bhopi and Saurajit have simplified intimidating concepts and distilled them down to the essence of what is *really* important about the interrelationship between business and technology. They have served up these concepts in a consumable and relatable package. This book is ideal for the executive who finds IT to be otherwise a proverbial 'black box.' Read it to discover what *Demystifying IT* can do to transform how you think about technology. I hope you enjoy it as much as I did."

—Martin Jenns
Executive Vice President and President, Assurant Global Automotive

"This book is a must-read for CEOs. In a succinct and efficient way, it accomplishes the title: demystifying IT. That is only the beginning, because it leads to the true purpose and value of the book: it provides concrete advice and a roadmap for how to lead a company in utilizing technology as a strategic business tool, and how to avoid the pitfalls of failed or bogged-down technology projects. There are general business truths in this book that CEOs will already know, such as 'every company today is an IT company' and 'you must thrive to survive.' The authors describe in concise terms how to bridge those truths to reality for your company.

"I particularly enjoyed that the book is built on a deep understanding of business. One truth it brings home is that

IT people must understand the business, or IT projects within the company will fail. The gap between IT and businesspeople must be closed, and this book offers real-world solutions for how to do that, as well as insights into hiring the right IT people. The compelling content and real-world examples make this a top read for CEOs and executive teams across the company."

—Kathryn Koorenny
General Counsel and Managing Director, AlixPartners

"Bhopi Dhall has been solving computer engineering challenges since the days when it was a challenge just to produce a 1 or 0. This book is written from the collective wisdom of the company he founded as they've tackled the critical challenges of software development: management, design, innovation, and delivery. From their unique seat in the industry, the talented people of CG Infinity share the lessons they've learned over decades."

—Jim Smelley
Cofounder and CEO of Thought Ensemble;
Coauthor of *Reboot: Competing with Technology Strategy*

"I have lived this book. Today, I'm the vice president of customer experience at an IT consulting firm. I'm a technologist and a strategic bridge between IT and their counterparts in operations and sales. I've led, and seen, my fair share of transformations in the name of efficiency, cost-to-serve reductions, and customer experience improvements.

"But roughly half a decade ago when I met Saurajit Kanungo and later Bhopi, this was not the case. I was a quality manager then. My purpose was to improve the operations of our company's contact center. Studying trends found within contact-centered data, my team and I worked with operations leadership to make training-based and process changes that were supposed to help contact center personnel improve their metrics. It was a repetitive process that maintained the status quo but did very little to move the needle.

We had problems that wouldn't yield to our best efforts. Cost-to-serve remained high. The level of customer attrition was scary. We could see that within the data we had been mining, there was a potential roadmap to solutions. The data highlighted correlations to our problems, and if it could be fed as fuel into a processing engine, the output might dramatically enhance our contact center's capabilities. What we lacked was the right engine and people to help us operate it.

"Enter Saurajit and his team. Long story short: with their help we shaped our company's data and weaponized it for good. We created automations and automatons that helped our customers solve problems before they knew they had problems and allowed them access to our company and products without having to access our human resources. Customer experience went up; attrition and costs went down, and the company continues to innovate today—constantly iterating on what has been done previously for a continually better experience and EBITDA.

"Other results? Promotions and amazing new cutting-edge technology to work on and implement. Constant learning of new methods, management styles, and approaches to complex problem solving and cross-functional team design. A true partnership, in which the client company and the consultants shared benefits and became better.

"The work, the results, and the learnings were all so fantastic that today, I now work with Saurajit and Bhopi at CG Infinity—and am lucky enough to call them friends and mentors. Bhopi and Saurajit are IT sherpas. They are the Obi-Wan to your Luke Skywalker, the Gandalf to your Frodo or Bilbo; the kind of trustworthy guides who can help you to be heroic. They have built their knowledge throughout the evolution of IT, and they bring that to you. They help you further define your problem, then help you design your solution and give you the tools to build it. In the process, they create a partnership between IT and other parts of the business that weren't previously there.

"Now these wizards have distilled their experience and approaches into this book. It can act as your roadmap. Read the book."

—Mike Parish
Vice President of Customer Experience, CG Infinity

Demystifying IT

Bhopi Dhall and
Saurajit Kanungo

Demystifying IT

The Language of IT for the CEO

Forbes | Books

Published by Forbes Books, Charleston, South Carolina.
Member of Advantage Media.

Forbes Books is a registered trademark, and the Forbes Books colophon is a trademark of Forbes Media, LLC.

Printed in the United States of America.

10 9 8 7 6 5 4 3 2 1

ISBN: 978-1-95086-377-8 (Hardcover)
ISBN: 978-1-95588-475-4 (eBook)

LCCN: 2022922585

Cover design by Joshua Frederick.
Layout design by Wesley Strickland.

This custom publication is intended to provide accurate information and the opinions of the authors in regard to the subject matter covered. It is sold with the understanding that the publisher, Forbes Books, is not engaged in rendering legal, financial, or professional services of any kind. If legal advice or other expert assistance is required, the reader is advised to seek the services of a competent professional.

Since 1917, Forbes has remained steadfast in its mission to serve as the defining voice of entrepreneurial capitalism. Forbes Books, launched in 2016 through a partnership with Advantage Media, furthers that aim by helping business and thought leaders bring their stories, passion, and knowledge to the forefront in custom books. Opinions expressed by Forbes Books authors are their own. To be considered for publication, please visit **books.Forbes.com**.

Contents

Why to Read This Book + What's in It

For any of us, there are two kinds of knowledge: things we need to know and things that are nice to know. This is a need-to-know book. The messages and principles laid out in these pages add up to a survival guide for midsized companies in the digital age.

The stakes are high. With the ongoing spread of information technology, it's now fair to say that "every company is an IT company"—or needs to be. Time and again in our work with client companies, we've seen them prosper by tapping the full potential of IT. You'll read a few of their stories here. We also see companies get into deep trouble by failing to grasp or use the capabilities of IT properly. You'll read a few of these cautionary tales, too.

This book is written primarily for CEOs, owner/directors, and executives on the "business side" of midsized firms. Over on the so-called IT side, you have the CIO and other specialists. You don't need to understand all the mysterious technical details of what they do. But you and your business leaders definitely need to go beyond thinking of IT as merely an overhead expense. The IT toolkit is growing every day, affecting everything we do. *Winning in any industry requires a level of knowledge and awareness that will allow you to leverage that toolkit to the max.*

> **Winning in any industry requires a level of knowledge and awareness that will allow you to leverage that toolkit to the max.**

In the pages ahead, we'll show you ways in which IT can be used for breaking into new markets, offering new or upgraded products and services, streamlining operations, and improving customer acquisition and retention—these being some of the main aspects that impact the bottom line.

And there's another key ingredient to winning. The company's business side has to work in true partnership with the IT side. Treating the IT team essentially as order-takers, by giving them requests and requirements and expecting them to turn out results, is a recipe for miscommunication and, in many cases, disaster. The relationship needs to be deeply collaborative from square one.

For this reason, we strongly encourage IT leaders to read the book as well. While it's natural for anyone to focus on what they do best (especially if it is their designated responsibility!), we find that too often, this tendency limits the top people on the IT side. They settle into the order-taking role. They don't get a seat at the table for strategic planning and decision making because they don't demand it. And without their input the company is limited in its ability to exploit IT. The collaboration has to work both ways. We think this book can help IT leaders to understand and speak the language of their colleagues on the business side, so the company can thrive.

The rest of the book breaks out as follows.

- The first two chapters bring you "into the IT-verse." They explain and illustrate basic concepts for navigating an IT-intensive business world. You also get a simple scorecard-type chart for assessing where your company stands in the race.

- Chapters 3 through 6 offer true stories to learn from. Each chapter gives you an in-depth look, with our analysis, at how an actual midsized company has leveraged IT for dramatic growth and profit. The stories cover a range of industries. They show different ways of putting IT to work, along with some common good-practice principles that underlie all of them.

- Chapters 7 and 8 are devoted to building a good working relationship between the business and IT leaders of a company. Here you'll find basic principles combined with specific nuts-and-bolts steps for making the collaboration sing.

- Chapter 9's title, "A Roadmap to the Future," speaks for itself. We hope you will use this book as a springboard for taking action: for doing what's needed to move your company to the front of the race in business IT. Therefore, our send-off chapter offers a suggested template around which to build a strategic action plan.

And that's it. If you are on board, let's begin the journey.

CHAPTER 1:

Into the IT-Verse

T he aha moment came for young Miles Morales when he fell from a high window. To his amazement, he was able to break his fall by grabbing—and sticking to—the sheer side of the building. The girl named Eleven knew she was telekinetic but didn't realize how strong the force field was until she focused her gaze on a pursuing van full of bad guys. The vehicle flipped in the air and crashed while Eleven, on a bicycle, raced ahead.

These scenes from *Spider-Man: Into the Spider-Verse* and *Stranger Things* are examples of a classic action-story theme: people discovering that they have a superpower. Can it happen in business? Yes indeed. Maybe not as dramatically, but often with equally great effects. We have worked with midsized companies that defied gravity in falling markets, outraced the competition, and launched themselves into new surges of growth. In each case, they did it by learning to tap a power that was at their fingertips all along: information technology.

There are times when IT actually does seem magical. You have probably heard that the phone you carry has more computing capacity than all of NASA had when it sent men to the moon in 1969. Furthermore, whereas NASA's IT systems performed a strictly defined set of tasks, you can put your little phone to work in almost countless ways. It can find parking spots where there don't seem to be any. You can use it to teleconference, trade stocks, or translate Greek.

Very few of us today would consider using a phone only to make phone calls. And yet, it is all too easy for companies to get stuck in a similar phase of stalled development by underutilizing the powers of IT. For a company in this stage, the IT department exists mainly as a support function. The IT staff are expected to keep the local network running, troubleshoot when somebody can't get their bits and bytes to behave—those kinds of things.

And if you were to look at the company's financials, you would find a telltale sign. The IT budget is listed under general and administrative costs, which means it is being treated as overhead. In this "G&A stage," as we call it, a great technology of our times is viewed as just a necessary expense—another utility, like water and electric—when, in fact, IT is the single best lever a company can grasp to launch new business ideas, leverage up income, and leverage down costs across the board.

But let's make one thing clear. No shame or fault is attached to being in the G&A stage. For many companies, it is a natural stage on the road to IT growth. What is important is not to stay in it. Here are some sneak previews of stories to be told more fully a bit later. They are true stories of midsized companies with revenues ranging from around $100 million to a few billion per year that have capitalized on the leverage of IT.

- In a series of planned steps, a community bank redid both the back-office and customer-facing aspects of its IT infrastructure. The moves had multiple benefits. This traditional, local consumer bank was better able to compete with sophisticated players, like the big multistate banks and new e-banks. Moreover, armed with scalable IT, the bank acquired numerous other banks of its type—rolling them into the same IT platform and becoming a regional force, instead of an endangered relic.

- A manufacturer of automated welding rigs saw the new wave coming. Factory equipment like theirs could no longer just run automatically. It had to be intelligent, capable of being reprogrammed or self-adjusting on the fly. With the aid of our founder, Bhopi Dhall, the company built digital intelligence into its welding machines. They're now used in motor-vehicle assembly plants and other types of factories internationally.

- Meanwhile, some companies jump ahead of the wave. One that we've worked with, an electricity trading company, mediates contracts between providers of electric power and commercial/institutional users. By digitizing the process on a Web platform, the company migrated from lengthy back-and-forth haggling over potential contracts to rapid, IT-driven matching of buyers with sellers on optimum terms. Now try a couple of softball questions: Do you think this attracted more business? Did the company grow by quantum leaps while cutting costs and improving margins?

A couple of disclaimers are in order. Not every midsized firm that embraces the leverage of IT will grow through the roof. Some have to be content with moderate growth, making various improvements that add up to a measurable gain in EBITDA … and that enable them to survive in fast-changing times. If that is sufficient to encourage you to read on, please do.

Also, please be aware that we are not trying to sell you the services of our firm. Frankly, our purpose in writing this book does include a vanity component. Our experience with IT for business use is deep and broad. We would like to be seen as thought leaders. But the broader purpose is to help you be a leader—or, more accurately, the best you can be.

Unsung Heroes

Our hearts are especially warmed by speaking with midsized companies in the millions-to-a-few-billions range. For one thing, these companies tend to have high potential for using IT to a greater extent than they typically do. They're often generating or collecting tons of data, which is *actionable information* that can be used for improving the business or even changing how the company does business—if it is used correctly.

And there is a deeper reason. Midsized companies are crucial to this nation's well-being. People tend to think our economy runs on the strength of the big firms: the acronym companies like GE, GM, IBM, and 3M, along with newer tech giants like Amazon, Apple, and Google. Certainly, these organizations do important work, and they employ many people. But no country can have an economy that consists only of big firms. It would be like an ecosystem of nothing but elephants. There are thousands of goods and business functions that have to be provided by companies in just the bracket that we've described: big and experienced enough to do it really well and the right size to be able to focus on serving particular niches.

Midsized companies do all the work in between the massive stuff and what gets done by small local contractors, doctors' offices, and so forth. They are human-scale companies with the ability to make human life better for many of us. *They are the unsung heroes of our economy.* And to the extent they can leverage their human intelligence with IT intelligence, everybody benefits.

The rest of this chapter explores how companies can get diverted from being their best, along with how technology in general—and information technology in particular—has become such an important factor.

The IT Traps (and How to Avoid Them)

There are two main reasons that many companies stay trapped in the G&A phase of treating IT as overhead.

1. *The executive team and the board haven't yet had their aha moment.* The business has been doing fine as it is. Not wishing to fix what doesn't look broken, the leaders do little more than make tweaks and marginal updates. They simply don't perceive the opportunity cost of chances foregone, since it doesn't show up in the financials. (Have you ever seen a line item for opportunity cost?) They also may not appreciate the dangers of gradually lagging behind the competition or being caught unprepared by disruptive change.

2. *The executives and board have had an "oh no" moment.* Sometime in the recent past, they decided to go all-in for state-of-the-art IT. Perhaps the company invested millions to implement an enterprise software package from a major vendor, and it turned into a major boondoggle. The project ran over schedule and over budget. Consultants were buzzing

around, racking up fees while they interfered with the flow of business. Worse, the system never really worked right or delivered the capabilities it was supposed to. If you talk to such a company about leveraging IT, the gut response will likely be "We're not going down that rabbit hole again."

A disaster of this kind would make anyone feel wary, though it is hardly surprising. Surveys across industries show that 70 to 80 percent of ERP implementations fail to achieve their objectives. The statistics look similarly discouraging for so-called digitization projects—the more creative, ambitious kind—which are meant to boost sales and profits by digitizing a product, a service, or a new business model. Very often, the great leap forward comes apart in midleap. The company winds up more traumatized than digitized.[1]

We've been called in more than once on rescue missions by companies looking for someone to help them put Humpty Dumpty back together. The good news is that usually the system can be gotten into reasonable working order. The sad news is that many companies misconceive what went wrong in the first place.

When a big project fails, there is a tendency to blame the technology. Complex new IT systems come to be seen as a sort of tease to be avoided—the kind that promise big thrills but will leave you stung. So naturally the lesson seems to be "Don't touch that hot wire anymore." But the problem is not the technology. The problem is the execution.

The problem is not the technology. The problem is the execution.

Here are two common sources of project failure, along with key steps that can turn them into positives.

---

1   See, for example, Corrie Block, "12 Reasons Your Digital Transformation Will Fail," *Forbes*, March 16, 2022, https://www.forbes.com/sites/forbescoachescouncil/2022/03/16/12-reasons-your-digital-transformation-will-fail/?sh=a101fc21f1ee.

- **PROBLEM:** There are fundamental disconnects between the business leaders and IT leaders in the company. They don't understand each other's fields very well, nor do they collaborate fully or well. Since the purpose of the project is to leverage IT to achieve business goals, this is a recipe for ill-conceived planning up front, followed by friction and fracture along the way.

  SOLUTION: The two "sides" of the company need to be in sync from day one. Key business strategists and department heads must get a good basic grasp of what can and cannot be done with information technology. Conversely, the CIO or other such person must do likewise in terms of grasping business strategies. Then the various parties must work together closely as a true leadership *team*. All of that can be a tall order, and only one executive has the clout to make it happen. The CEO must take on the role of coordinator-in-chief.

- **PROBLEM:** Too much complexity in one bite. Usually, it doesn't work well to attempt an extreme IT makeover or an ambitious digitization project in one big jump. Even a relatively simple system is very complex. Beneath the staggering number of lines of code in a software program, there's an even more staggering number of 1s and 0s, the basic binary language that machines can understand. Therefore, when you create or install a large software package—which requires integrating the many moving parts to meet your company's specific needs—you are juggling layers upon layers of complexity. This vastly multiplies the odds that some bits and pieces won't come together right until the whole edifice begins to crack and crumble.

SOLUTION: The way to deal with complexity is to divide and conquer. For any major project, we recommend laying out a master plan and then breaking it into actionable chunks. Each chunk should itself produce a tangible benefit to the company, such as automating a task. Or providing data and prompts for customer retention or adding a key strategic functionality; you name it. Only when and if each job is done properly do you spend on the next. You can rethink or stop at any stage and still come away with new IT leverage that gives the business a boost.

Of course, other sources of trouble may arise, but these are the big ones. We see them so frequently that they seem to be chronic, endemic issues. Left unaddressed, their effects can be massively negative. The good news is that the solutions, when properly applied, become powerful enablers.

Now Where Do We Go from Here?

Thus far, we have offered you a general overview of the potential and pitfalls of information technology for business.

The next chapter, chapter 2, will present a simple framework that shows how a midsized company can literally "climb the ladder" in IT capability—from using the technologies only for routine internal needs to leveraging them for maximum impact.

That chapter, along with a few more, will tell real-life case stories. You'll see how midsized companies in different industries with different strategic goals have done the right things and dodged the wrong moves to get digital technology taking them where they want to go.

The need to align the business and IT sides of the company is foundational. So, while the case stories include glimpses of how this can be done, two entire chapters near the end—chapters 7 and 8—tackle the subject in depth.

Meanwhile, let's see how much good we can do by wrapping up this chapter. First, we'll step back in time to trace a (very) brief history of information technology. Historical context is always helpful. None of us lives on an island in time. In the story of how IT has evolved, it's possible to see parallels to how a present-day company can evolve and grow along similar lines.

And *that* message is brought home in the closing section.

IT in a Nutshell—from Basic Calculations to Core Capabilities

Computers were first designed, literally, to compute: to run long calculations faster than math wizards could. But it soon became apparent that they were capable of more. One person who saw this was the British scientist Alan Turing. During World War II, he worked on the Ultra project, which used crude part-electric, part-mechanical computing equipment to decipher messages that the Nazis encoded with their Enigma machines. The task was very difficult because not only were Enigma codes complex, they kept changing. Each message had to be decrypted separately, and with computing help, they were.

And here is the aha point: although codebreaking is a mathematical sort of problem, the end result is to solve a language problem. What the computer does is more like what Google Translate does today—reading text in a "foreign" language and writing it out in your own. Alan Turing and others quickly jumped on this insight and extended it. If a computer could "read" and "write," couldn't it also be rigged up to listen and speak?

The idea wasn't far-fetched at all. During the same early years of World War II, British scientists deployed another new form of IT: radar. A line of radar towers called the Chain Home system was built along the coast of England. The towers could detect incoming Nazi aircraft in time for the Royal Air Force to scramble a response, which helped England survive the Blitz. And radar was a method of seeing or, if you prefer, "hearing" things that eyes and ears could not.

Piece by piece, the potential IT toolkit began to grow, along with the notion of a so-called general-purpose computer that could be put to almost any task. And with this came the realization that IT was a *competitive advantage* that could be leveraged in multitudes of ways. In the postwar years, it became standard for every sizable business to have a computer or at least access to one. American computer makers like Sperry and IBM came to the fore, while the US Defense Department took a big lead in funding and conducting research. The military was sold on putting technology at the core of its efforts. Never again could generals tell R&D geeks that their ideas were interesting but irrelevant.

In the late 1960s, the Defense Department's Defense Advanced Research Projects Agency funded the building of the ARPANET, a network for linking computers across long distances so they could communicate by wire. The ARPANET would grow and evolve, taking on a life of its own. Today it's known as the internet.

Permit us now to bring ourselves into the story. Around 1970, coauthor Bhopi had immigrated from India and was working as a young electrical engineer at Texas Instruments. Along with building a robot as a side project, he worked on TI's Advanced Scientific Computer. The ASC was one of the first supercomputers to use vector processing, of which there is no need to understand the details. Suffice it to say that the same approach was used by Seymour Cray in his more famous Cray supercomputers, which for many years were the standard for working on very hard scientific problems.

Skip ahead now to the late 1990s. Personal computers, linked together instead of operating as standalones, have become the new way to go. They're running software for everything from graphic design to game-playing. Computer modeling—the use of IT to emulate a real-life situation so it can be analyzed and various actions can be tried to see how they might work out—has advanced to the point where it's applied regularly in business planning and many other areas: IBM's Deep Blue chess-playing system proved it could beat a grandmaster.

And, of course, the public World Wide Web has become a global phenomenon. Bhopi, by this time, has founded his own company. He is using the Web in applications for clients' industrial control systems and also, bit by bit, for IT systems in business. The ecommerce wave gradually brings an increasing focus on the latter. With the advent of smart mobile phones, those get integrated into the picture too. In 2010—to dwell just a bit more on our own experience—coauthor Saurajit joins Bhopi's company. Saurajit had previously been a chartered accountant in India, where his big project was computerizing the accounting systems for a public entity operating five international airports. He's also been part of a couple of fast-growing business-system startups in the United States. With his arrival, Bhopi's company is almost exclusively dedicated to the business clientele it currently serves.

Bringing the state of IT up to where it stands today would require a few books longer than we are writing. Instead, let's close this chapter by focusing on a core message.

Every Company Is Now an IT Company

Or to state it more bluntly: every company now *needs to be* an IT company and to act accordingly, or else risk being left in the dust.

In the past, it was just common sense for businesses to define themselves by what they made or sold. A shoemaker made shoes. Fishmongers sold fish. Ford Motor Company made motor vehicles, and so forth. In the second half of the twentieth century, as some big corporations began to be put out of business by newer technologies, management scholars suggested that they ought to define their purpose and identity more fundamentally. For example, maybe if railroad companies had said, "We're in the transportation business" instead of "We run trains," they'd have found ways to compete better with airlines and trucking companies. Or maybe if Blockbuster had said, "We deliver home entertainment" instead of "We rent videos," the company would still be around and doing all the things that Netflix does.

Information technology has become so ubiquitous and so powerful that the potential to use it proactively in every area of business simply cannot be ignored.

But now, in our view, that form of definition also needs to be amended. Information technology has become so ubiquitous and so powerful that the potential to use it proactively in every area of business simply cannot be ignored. It has become a central fact of life—for companies, for customers, for people.

And therefore, we argue, the new realistic common sense is to start from the technology. "We're an IT company that uses IT, intelligently, to sell fish"—or to sell furniture, insurance, or anything else. Let us give you an example. Although we don't normally like to offer big-company examples to midsized companies, the Amazon story is well worth learning from.

Why did Amazon begin as an online bookstore? Not because Jeff Bezos loves books, although he's been known to read them. It was because he had a *technology* idea—a vision of a Web platform for selling all kinds of goods, one that would leverage the reach and efficiency of IT—and he was looking for the best product to start with for testing and building out the idea. He chose books as an ideal product for selling online: people don't need to try them on to see if they fit. Books do not spoil; they have no fragile parts to worry about in shipping, and customer returns are rare. *The technology drove the business.*

In fact, technology also turned out to be the most valuable *part* of the business. What is Amazon's most profitable line of sales today? It's not books or clothing or consumer electronics. It is Amazon Web Services: the cloud computing and storage service that grew out of IT infrastructure that the company first developed for its own use. In 2021, AWS accounted for only about 13 percent of Amazon's gross revenue but over 54 percent of the operating profit. It's a case of selling your own technology to others. And Amazon was far from the first company to do such a thing.

Back in the 1960s, there was a steel fabrication plant in South Carolina making things like the lightweight steel joists that hold up the roofs in shopping malls. The owners had trouble getting decent steel stock at affordable prices, so they tried a bit of a gamble. They had learned of a steelmaking technology called an electric arc furnace, which was said to be much cheaper and more cost-effective than the processes used by the major steel companies. The plant owners decided they would build their own little "minimill" to become self-sufficient. Soon they were rolling light steel beams and bars for other fabricators too. And they've long since left their original fabrication business. Today, Nucor is the largest steelmaker in the United States, with over twenty IT-controlled minimills across the country.

You don't have to be nearly as big as Amazon or Nucor to do this. We know of a midsized regional service company that used IT to intelligently automate part of its operations. As this book was being written, the company was considering whether to lease the platform to other companies of its type. By doing so they might lose some of the edge they've had over the competition, but if the earnings from leasing their IT would make up the difference plus a lot more—which apparently it would—then they will come out well on top of the game.

The company has learned a couple of key lessons from this chapter. IT is a lever, not overhead. And acting like an IT company is the best way to *get* ahead.

Now we will see how intelligent, proactive use of information technology can impact every line of EBITDA.

CHAPTER 2:

Impacting EBITDA: Step by Step, Line by Line

There is an old story—probably part fact and part legend—about a super-strongman in the days of ancient Greece. At the Olympic games, he was the wrestler nobody could defeat. He was a fearsome warrior. He was generally the man to call whenever heavy lifting was needed. And how did Milo of Croton grow so strong?

It is said that when Milo was a boy living on a farm, one day he was present at the birth of a baby ox. Delighted, he picked up the newborn calf and carried it around to show to everyone. The next day he did it again. And the next, and the next. By the time the calf had matured, he could lift a one-ton draft animal, and the rest is history.

We don't know how much of this tale is true. Verification is beyond the scope of Snopes. But the story offers a template for how a company can grow strong in the use of information technology.

Step by step is the way to go. When it comes to leveraging IT, most midsized companies begin from a state of relative infancy. The trick is to build gradually through focused initiatives that lift performance in one area of the business and then the next and the next. As you do this, you get into a growth groove. You're always reaching to do more than you did yesterday but never taking on more than you can handle.

If you plan with foresight and execute well—with the support of outside IT services, as needed, to complement your own capabilities—progress will show up as impacts on each major line of the financials. Ultimately, companies that go for peak returns may find they can move mountains.

This chapter spells out the particulars in two sections. The first outlines a typical course of step-by-step progression. Then comes a case study of a midsized specialty company that has achieved the ultimate.

Four Stages of IT Leverage

Through long experience, we have come up with a rating system that ranks midsized companies by how far they have advanced in using IT to impact every line of EBITDA. You don't need to be a computer scientist to understand these ratings. There are four simple categories: Crawl, Walk, Run, and Fly.

TABLE 2-1: RANKING COMPANIES BY IT USE

		CRAWL	WALK	RUN	FLY
Admin and Support Uses	Basic IT for internet, email, etc.	Yes	Yes	Yes	Yes
Sales and Marketing	Leverage IT to grow or maintain top line		Yes	Yes	Yes
Cost of Goods Sold	Reduce cost of goods sold, improve gross profit margin			Yes	Yes
Expansion, Exponential Growth	Use IT to enter new markets, Blue Oceans				Yes

Chances of marketplace survival increase by moving this way. >>

EBITDA is likely to grow by moving this way. >>

CRAWL—About 80 percent of midsized companies are in the elementary stage of IT use. The technologies are used as normal day-to-day working tools: for accounting, for internet access and email, and so forth. The IT department plays a support role to keep systems and devices running. Nearly all of the IT budget shows up as an overhead expense under G&A.

It's not a total loss to be at this stage, since almost any use of IT will produce some efficiencies. Digital messages and documents do not have to be physically delivered. Looking up information online is usually quicker than thumbing through reference materials. But even for these basic functions, we find that many companies fall short of using IT optimally. For example, internal systems may not be set up so that team members can easily get vital information on items like inventory levels or the status of a project.

A smart teenager with a smartphone could probably get a wider range of benefits from her IT than some of these companies are getting from theirs. And at their present pace, they are greatly at risk of falling behind sophisticated competitors, which is why we say they're operating at a crawl.

WALK—Perhaps 10 to 15 percent of companies have stepped up to this stage in recent years. They have begun to *leverage* IT for top-line growth, typically in sales and marketing. They have a functioning CRM system and use it for at least the minimum benefits that it can provide. CRM's most basic benefit is simply recording and centralizing information on customers, prospects, and leads. If a top sales rep quits, this assures that the person won't walk away with your best contacts.

A properly used system also can help mediocre salespeople get better. They're able to go into a potential selling situation guided by a screen that displays a wealth of data about the customer. In retail banking, for example, there might be personal information that helps to build a personal relationship—and along with the customer's financial profile and history, it could provide cues for talking about any number of products: home equity loans, retirement accounts, or financing for the children's education. Similarly, in a B2B environment, the system can help with onboarding a prospect, cross-selling, and more. Whereas the best salespeople learn on their own how to gather and use certain kinds of knowledge, CRM *institutionalizes* the knowledge and makes it accessible in ways that can raise overall performance.

Companies that leverage this capability are starting to walk the walk of the IT age. They may also have digital marketing efforts that go beyond "let's try Google Ads," and/or a website that actually helps to sell rather than just taking orders or linking people to sales reps.

They're seeing top-line revenue growth or at least not losing ground in that regard. Customer acquisition and retention look better than before. Competitively, these companies hover around the middle of the pack in their markets, with room to move ahead.

RUN—Companies in the vanguard, about 5 to 10 percent of the total, tap the power of IT to reduce their cost of goods sold. They are putting out more work more efficiently, with fewer people or resources, or both. The details of how this is done may vary depending on the industry, but the companies' financial statements tend to show the same pattern. Their ability to grow the top line while paring down the COGS line gives them significant bottom-line gains.

Further, these companies tend to do better than most at growing the top line. In addition to getting maximum impact from CRM, they have digital marketing campaigns that go quite far beyond traditional approaches in precision and reach. Their websites are designed to be active sales tools. Their analytics enable them to measure the cost-effectiveness of new marketing tactics so they can improve and grow systematically, attributing gains to specific causes and actions.

These companies also master the use of IT in delivering customer satisfaction at every point of contact. The so-called customer experience is hard to get right, and it's a vital part of the picture. We'll say more about it shortly. The point for now is that companies in this stage are firing on all cylinders. By leveraging IT throughout the organization, they run at the pace of a market leader. By judiciously mixing contracted IT services with a lean and efficient in-house staff, they're able to keep upgrading and tweaking their IT systems to stay ahead of the pack. They have achieved a *sustainable competitive advantage*.

And there is one more level to be reached.

FLY—Companies that shift into the highest gear literally take off. Equipped with all-around IT competence, they go on the offensive in terms of corporate strategy, aiming to clearly separate themselves from the ground-dwellers in their field.

Often they adopt a Blue Ocean strategy, expanding into new market niches or new territories where few if any competitors have ventured as yet. A classic example of a company that's done this consistently is Netflix.

Recall that Netflix began, in 1997, by mailing DVDs of movies to people's homes on a rental basis. The company's original IT advantage was that you could rent a movie on their website instead of going to a physical storefront. But even at that early stage, the plan was not simply to do a Web-based end run around Blockbuster. As one report on the company's history pointed out: "Netflix knew DVDs would be anachronistic years before Internet streaming was invented."[2]

By the time streaming was commercially feasible in 2007, Netflix was geared up to exploit it. This in turn sustained rapid growth and built the financial clout to jump to the next level. In 2013, Netflix expanded from distribution of streaming content into content creation, with Netflix Originals. The *House of Cards* series was the first, to be followed by many more. And while many companies have the resources to create video series and feature films, few have developed audience analytics to the level Netflix has. An old Hollywood adage says that "nobody knows anything" about what's going to be the next hit. Repeatedly in recent years, Netflix has proven the conventional wisdom wrong by

---

2   Alex Sherman, "Reed Hastings Won by Studying Amazon—Then Running in the Opposite Direction," CNBC, June 16, 2018, https://www.cnbc.com/2018/06/13/netflix-reed-hastings-inspiration-amazon.html.

pinpointing the conception and content of its Originals to specific audience segments and marketing them accordingly.

* * *

There are plenty of good chess players but not many grandmasters. One thing they have learned to do is to think more moves ahead than the average person does. And so it is in IT. The technologies keep advancing. By staying on top of what is possible while keeping an eye out for opportunities to leverage the art of the possible, you can fly.

Now let's see how a midsized company, much smaller and less known than Netflix, has leveraged IT to soar far beyond its previous bounds. We are keeping the company's name anonymous, but if you are familiar with the industry, you may guess who it is.

> *The technologies keep advancing. By staying on top of what is possible while keeping an eye out for opportunities to leverage the art of the possible, you can fly.*

Midsized Company, Outsized Success

Company A is a major player in a specialty niche: precious metals trading. The company is among the relatively few authorized to buy gold, silver, and platinum directly from the US Mint and other mints in the form of specially struck coins and bars that are authenticated for high precious-metal content. Upon making its purchases, the company acts as a broker, selling the goods to retail dealers. The dealers then sell to customers who want the coins and bars as collectibles, investments, or both.

Brokering anything can be a hectic business. As of 2016—the year before a major IT upgrade—Company A had a staff of about thirty traders who were constantly phoning, emailing, and faxing with dealers located around the world. It was an old-school approach with old-school problems. Tracking inventory in real time to avoid promising the same limited stock to two or more buyers was a recurring issue. Orders were shipped without auto-tracing, and sometimes valuable packages went missing.

Company A also has a parallel business, a refinery for extracting precious metals from old jewelry, dental scrap, and such. To coordinate everything, the owners were using a patchwork of ERP systems implemented over the years. This IT infrastructure did not function well. Altogether, operations were costly and inefficient. Competitors operated in similar ways, but the level playing field didn't help much. On both the trading side and the refinery side, Company A's markets combined the toughest features of a commodity business and a luxury business. Price competition was fierce, and quality of service mattered too.

By 2016, the owners had reached a point where business as usual no longer looked attractive. To go on competing in years ahead, they'd have to accept lower profit margins, which already were shaved thinner than one would like. So they called on our firm to see if further efficiencies could be gained from IT. And after thorough analysis, an even better option emerged.

A series of major changes, done in carefully planned steps, had the potential to do more than cut some costs here and there. They could add up to a quantum leap forward, equipping Company A with state-of-the-art operations and clear advantages over the rest of the field. Ownership gave the green light, and work began.

- A key step was redoing the website so that most clients, most of the time, could order online. It was made possible because the company was open to rethinking how it worked. Precious metals trading is a business built on trust. Traditionally, this was thought to require personal contact and attention. But, in fact, trust comes from executing transactions reliably, efficiently, and easily at a fair price. Modern IT—when designed and implemented well—can do those things better than a small army of traders working the phones.

Prior to the redo, only a minority of trades were done online. The website had been set up mainly to display current offerings and then link the visitor to a trading rep by email or voice. The redesign flipped the script. Orders placed online jumped to about 90 percent of total sales volume. The times when dealers really wanted or needed personal interaction turned out to be exceptions, not the rule.

One year after the new website went up, Company A's staff of thirty traders was reduced to eight. By three years out, just two traders were handling calls and emails promptly. For a firm where this department had once been a significant fraction of overall headcount, the cost savings were huge. And the savings had been gained without compromising service. Indeed, customers liked the new system better.

- APIs were installed so that dealers could link their own IT systems with Company A's. This made their purchasing and accounting easier all around. It enabled them to choose their method of delivery and trace shipments automatically, from a mobile app if desired.

- A separate section of the new Company A website devoted to the refining business enabled online ordering with the same benefits for refinery customers.

- Meanwhile, the company's entire IT infrastructure was being streamlined and updated step by step. These back-end improvements gave managers and employees greater visibility and control over all operations—from warehousing and fulfillment to marketing and more. Efficiency improved across the board, cutting G&A expenses generally and reducing costs of goods sold for both the trading business and the refinery. Eventually, the company was able to sunset its legacy ERP packages for inventory and logistics, keeping only what integrated well with the new system.

- A significant step in boosting top-line impact was to ramp up digital marketing. Integration with Google Analytics allowed Company A to target online ads with good precision and attract new customers in greater numbers more easily than before.

- Ultimately—by combining smart use of IT with market awareness—the company began to *create new revenue streams*. For example, wealthy individuals and institutional investors often want to include precious metals in their portfolios. So Company A built a Web platform for this purpose. Mutual fund managers and private investment advisors can tap into the platform to obtain plug-and-play IRA packages or other portfolio modules that fit their clients' needs. This service was the first of its kind in precious metals trading, and it has proved to be quite popular.

None of the above required a single, big, bet-the-company investment. All of it came from a carefully drawn up master plan accomplished in logical steps that fit together piece by piece. The results impacted EBITDA line by line, totaling very substantial gains on the bottom line.

And in the process, the company's competitive posture was utterly transformed. No longer is the firm caught in a race to the bottom, with perpetually squeezed margins. Company A is now the standard-setter for its industry. It has moved from shrinkage mode to expansion mode, riding increased revenues and profits while it explores Blue Oceans of new customers that competitors still struggle to reach.

Flying High, Continued

That's the power of leveraging IT. Step by step, line by line. Keeping a big goal in view while building practically and building in tune with the realities of changing markets. We recommend this approach because we have seen it work time and again, including for companies in lines of business quite different from precious metals.

The next few chapters show how several midsized firms in diverse industries leveraged IT to make order-of-magnitude leaps. We begin with the story of a community bank. This bank morphed from being an endangered species to a regional market dominator.

CHAPTER 3:

"Thrive to Survive": How a (Formerly) Small Bank Is Doing IT

One of the sharpest observers of modern technology—and one of the oddest—was Neil Postman, a longtime professor at New York University. An eloquent fellow with a big smile, Dr. Postman was often a guest on national TV shows. Yet for many years he didn't even own a TV. And although he lived and worked into the twenty-first century, Postman did not use the internet. Or a computer. Or a typewriter.

He probably kept a secretary very busy. It seems that as much as possible, Postman tried to be an impartial observer—watching the effects of modern tech without letting them influence his own thinking. He had noticed how powerful those effects can be. Here is an excerpt from a famous speech he gave.

*Technological change is not additive; it is ecological. I
can explain this best by an analogy. What happens if we
place a drop of red dye into a beaker of clear water? Do
we have clear water plus a spot of red dye? Obviously not.
We have a new coloration to every molecule of water. That
is what I mean by ecological change. A new medium does
not add something. It changes everything.*

This is what information technology is doing. IT has changed,
and continues to change, every aspect of every human ecosystem. If
your ecosystem is "business," it changes how your
customers and employees behave (or can behave). It
changes the playing field by altering time and space.
It changes the rules of competitive engagement.

> **IT has changed,
> and continues
> to change,
> every aspect of
> every human
> ecosystem.**

And for many companies, this presents an odd
problem. The company's leaders know that all of
the above is true. They see, and may even worry
about, IT affecting daily life on every level, from
young people absorbed in their phone screens to
news stories about the global impacts of IT. But
when it comes to changing their business strategies accordingly, they
get stuck, typically at some partway point somewhere in the range of
the Crawl and Walk stages described in the last chapter.

That will not do. The company becomes like a kayaker who loses
courage in heavy rapids, trying to cling to a boulder in the middle
of a fast-moving stream. It is not a sustainable strategy for survival.
When the forces of change are frothing and thundering all around,
as they now are in every industry, survival indeed is at stake. And just
as economists have recognized that there is no such thing as static
equilibrium in a market, a company must act on the fact that static

refuge isn't an option. You must pick a course through the rapids, make moves, and keep moving.

There is a simple way to put the message. Leaving metaphors and analogies aside, we find that in practically every industry today, the following is true:

YOU MUST THRIVE TO SURVIVE.

Traditionally, shifting a company into "survival mode" meant adopting a sort of bunker mentality. You trimmed expenses to the bare bones; maybe you closed a few branches. Any ideas pertaining to growth, ambition, or risk pretty much went on the shelf for the time being. Survival meant focusing on your so-called core business: defending your niche while mining the existing customer base for all it's worth.

The concept has some useful pieces, but as a whole, it is no longer viable. Today, the hunkering-down mode has become a last resort. It's what troubled companies do when revenues and resources shrink to the point where they can't afford to do much else. At best, it may give you enough of a cash runway to get through a temporary rough stretch—say, a recession or another pandemic, provided that neither lasts too long. But even then, you are subject to being buffeted and battered by other companies rushing past you.

The smartest companies are proactive. They play to win instead of trying not to lose. They take action well before they are squeezed down into the bunker of little hope, and their actions aim beyond their existing turf. They're looking for new customers, new markets, new revenue streams, and new ways to amplify what they already have. Their targets keep moving as times change. The company itself becomes a moving target, less vulnerable to attack by the competition.

Moreover, in all respects, their strategies go hand in hand with the ever-growing, ever-changing reach of information technology. They stay alert to new developments in IT that could threaten their business … and they're always implementing IT in new ways that can help the business.

Let's see how the executives at one midsized company are doing it. They could truly be called hometown heroes of the Information Age. The story is true in every detail. Only the company's name is fictional.

Go Big, Go Nimble: The Tale of a Very Friendly Bank

Few industries have been impacted more profoundly by IT than retail banking. Here and there you can still find banks that resemble those of a few decades ago: the majestic, pillared entrance. Inside, the massive steel-clad door to the safe deposit vault. A long row of tellers dealing face-to-face with local folks; the soothing sounds of paper money being counted out and coins jingling.

But this picture has ceased to be the norm. IT is changing the game in each of the broad senses that we've mentioned.

- **CUSTOMER BEHAVIOR**—Fewer people today are paid in bills and coins. Fewer use physical money for their personal spending; most don't even like to carry wallets full of cards or write checks. Local customer bases are less constant, as more people move and travel more. Younger people in particular like to bank from their phones—they'll visit the nearest branch bank for a special purpose, but otherwise avoid it—and the financial products that are popular have changed. Non-interest-bearing "Christmas Club" accounts have gone the way of the wooly mammoth. Modern financial shoppers expect menus of loan options, investment vehicles, and other instruments that give them a wide range of choices.

- **A CHANGED PLAYING FIELD, WITH ALTERATION OF TIME AND SPACE**—IT compresses time. Today's customers want instant access to instantly updated account information. Waiting for a monthly statement is *so* twentieth century. Transactions, too, are expected to be rapid, if not instant. (A bank wire on SWIFT takes two days? That's not swift!) As for boundaries of space, IT erases them. The home territory that you've nurtured for generations in a midwestern city is now open for business. An e-bank in California or a highly IT-enabled big bank elsewhere in the United States can swoop in through cyberspace and spirit customers away in minutes.

- **NEW RULES OF COMPETITIVE ENGAGEMENT**—Once upon a time, in any American city, you competed with a handful of similar banks located nearby. Now you compete with a world that includes other banks of various types, perhaps based half a continent away, and more. Online mortgage companies are blasting their television ads into people's homes. Investment and wealth-management companies are doing the same. Anyone shopping online will find popup buttons that offer deferred payment and financing plans, e-bundled in with their purchases if they so desire.

The list could go on and will probably have expanded by the time you read this. The point is that what used to be a gentlemanly boxing match is now more like MMA. You can be struck from an unexpected direction at any moment. And while changes in financial regulations have played a role in creating this environment, none of it could have happened without the enabler. The enabler—seeping ubiquitously through the mix, touching every molecule and making each one a bright-red hot spot, as in Dr. Postman's speech—is information technology.

The enabler–seeping ubiquitously through the mix, touching every molecule and making each one a bright-red hot spot–is information technology.

Smaller community and regional banks have been threatened the most by these changes. One that took the initiative to thrive, not just survive, was Friendly Bank (not its real name). Based in a medium-sized city near the center of the United States, Friendly had branches in smaller cities and towns throughout the metropolitan area plus some in outlying areas as well.

Leaders at Friendly Bank saw the IT wave coming early, during the first decade of the 2000s. They were especially concerned about being swept away by encroaching big banks like the Big Four (Chase, Citi, Bank of America, Wells Fargo). A strategic view indicated that Friendly should do several interrelated things to stay competitive.

One was to offer state-of-the-art services equal in quality and convenience to those offered by others. These would come to include new IT-based services, such as mobile check deposit and fund transfer, along with others that—once introduced—would soon be seen as baseline expectations by many customers.

The second requirement was to leverage IT internally, making operations more efficient and effective. Margins in consumer banking are thin. Friendly didn't have much margin for coasting, let alone for error.

Another was to stay nimble or, if possible, get nimbler than ever. The industry was sure to keep changing. Yesterday's SWOT analysis could quickly turn into ancient history. Here was another front where IT would be critical.

And to accomplish its goals, Friendly Bank would have to grow—bigger and faster than it had grown thus far. Size matters. One obvious way it can matter is by giving a company expanded market reach while walling off competitors. In Friendly's case, this would involve acquiring other good regional banks before they were snapped up and made into branches of a big megabank.

Just as important, size brings opportunities for improvements and efficiency gains across the board ... including in areas related to IT for consumer banking.

- One major benefit of digital technology is that software-based offerings, such as mobile apps, can be scaled to immense market size at very little added cost. Consider a feature like mobile check deposit. The cost of building and maintaining this feature will be pretty much the same whether you're a Big Four bank or a tiny one. But a big bank can offer the service to millions more customers, thereby enjoying a much lower per-unit cost of keeping customers happy.

- Additionally, as in any industry, consolidating back-office operations across a larger company can create economies of scale. This would further reduce Friendly Bank's cost of goods sold.

- Having more size and thus more purchasing power could also allow Friendly Bank to invest in bigger and better IT systems, thereby empowering all the other strategic steps that were seen as essential.

- Finally, while the changing environment was one in which Friendly could be struck from any direction, the reverse held true. Friendly itself could strike forth in new directions. The bank could explore the growing cyberworld of fintech, finding and tapping into new revenue streams. (For instance, by investing in newly available securities, as long as they were judged safe and complied with banking guidelines.) And this type of move, too, would be empowered by having greater size. The more assets a bank has under management, the more it's allowed to lend or invest.

So, growth was the word. The time to grow was as soon and as quickly as possible, given Friendly's resources. Starting around 2010—just as the economy was lifting out of the Great Recession— Friendly began a series of acquisitions, buying selected regional banks in both its home state and neighboring states. Some were rebranded as Friendly Bank while some with strong brand equity kept their own names but were rolled up into the Friendly family.

Solving an IT Bottleneck

Over the next few years, difficulties arose. Acquisitions went well, but the rollup process was slow and arduous. The acquired banks had an assortment of legacy IT systems, not all of which were first rate. On average, it was taking about a year to integrate each bank with Friendly's more advanced capabilities and to sunset the old systems. This amounted to a bottleneck in the Friendly growth trajectory. The pace of new acquisitions was bogging down. Expenses mounted; potential benefits took longer to materialize.

Friendly Bank had a long-term growth target of $60 billion in assets under management. At the existing pace, it wouldn't be possible to reach the target within the projected time frame, and meanwhile the clock was ticking. Time lost in the bottleneck would translate to missed revenue and lingering exposure to competitors. In 2016, the executive team called in our firm as consultants.

We began by sitting down with key leaders at Friendly and introspecting together on the last few acquisitions. Why was it taking so long to bring each bank into the Friendly system? How could we think and work differently to make things go faster? Our analysis led us to a fundamental realization. The best way to describe it in high-level terms without getting deep into technical details is this: we saw the need for a paradigm shift.

Friendly had been treating the process of adding a new bank as a systems integration problem. It would go much better if it were treated as a *data migration* problem. Here is the difference.

- By thinking in terms of systems integration, Friendly's people were setting themselves up for a job that amounted to a lot of customized plumbing. Each acquired bank's system had to be connected with the Friendly system so the two could work together while the Friendly system gradually took over and the old system was phased out. The connections that had to be made were complicated, and they were different every time.

- But all that really needed to happen, ultimately, was data migration. The acquired bank's customer data and user data had to be moved to Friendly's centralized system so the latter could manage and process all of it. Viewed this way, it was possible to design "migration processes" that would be semiautomated and repeatable. They'd be quicker to implement and essentially the same every time with a lot less custom pipefitting.

Now, making a paradigm shift of this type is easier said than done. There were challenges and constraints to consider. One of the *7 Habits of Highly Effective People* is "begin with the end in mind." And in Friendly Bank's case, a big endgame question arose. If the goal was to grow Friendly to several times its present size through acquisition, would Friendly's present IT infrastructure be able to handle several times its current load?

The answer was no. Any bank's IT "system," singular, is in fact an interwoven set of systems, plural, for various kinds of processing tasks. At the heart of it all is what bankers call the core system, which manages fund transfers, account balances, and so forth. Friendly's core system was scalable, but only to a certain extent. Beyond that, there might start to be slowdowns and possible breakdowns all through the systems.

So the first order of business, before tackling data migration, was to upgrade the core system and related systems linked with it—for online banking, mobile banking, and more. Fortunately, Friendly Bank had chosen a top-notch core system provider. This company did a fine job of giving us the required upgrade. As the other pieces came into place, we could start building the data migration processes.

The up-front work proved to be worth every penny. Instead of an integration process that took many months per acquired bank, we were able to design data-migration *routines*—as in, repeatable routines—that could be run in a couple of weeks. Even with the careful checking and verification work needed afterward—and even with the acquired bank's old system kept on life support for a while as a backup in case anything went wrong—the gains were dramatic.

Outcomes and Benefits

With this work, total time for integrating a newly acquired bank was reduced from a year to about one hundred days. Friendly ratcheted up its growth rate, able to acquire more and larger banks more quickly. At the latest count, in addition to the original Friendly Bank, the enterprise includes fourteen acquired banks in twelve metro areas across six states. The company is now firmly on track to meet its $60 billion assets target. And along the way, a host of expected benefits from size and consolidation are coming faster to fruition.

Services are more cost-effective. Staffing has been reduced in back offices and elsewhere throughout the Friendly Bank network, while skilled branch managers and relationship bankers who know their local markets have been kept in place at acquired banks—with better support than previously. The integrated 1-800 call center handles growing volumes of customer calls efficiently.

As new IT-based services are developed, they're able to be offered by all banks in the network promptly and simultaneously. That is better performance than any of the banks alone could typically achieve. For example, as we write this in 2022, more than a few independent regional banks have been late to the game in adding features, like the ability to handle Zelle payments. Others offer IT services that don't measure up quality-wise, like mobile check deposits with a clunky user interface reminiscent of the early internet. At banks operated by Friendly, customers get up-to-date services that sing on their latest phone screens.

Inside the banks, face-to-face customer service goes smoother and more productively. Relationship bankers at every branch can tap into Friendly Bank's centralized CRM system. As we explained in chapter 2, CRM is a force multiplier when well implemented. It coordinates and links a wealth of information on every customer. When a banker needs certain data for a customer sitting across the desk from her, she can call it up on her screen in a flash instead of rummaging around for the correct files. The system, on its own, is also constantly scanning the data it has stored, issuing prompts for opportunities to cross-sell and upsell. In between customer visits, the system helps bankers do their follow-up work more efficiently.

Results from this network-wide CRM access are measurable. At typical standalone regional banks, the average handling time for a walk-in customer visit may range from thirty minutes upward. Friendly-affiliated banks can send customers home happy, armed with the financial products and information they need, in ten to fifteen minutes.

ATM service often gets a boost too. Small regional banks with limited purchasing power usually buy from lower-echelon providers of ATM access. That's why their customers pay transaction fees when they are on the road and want to use an out-of-network machine. Customers of bigger regionals with more spending clout, like Friendly, tend to enjoy free ATM use over wider territories.

It's a minor convenience, to be sure. Customers who take advantage of expanded free ATM use might save a dollar to a few dollars per withdrawal. But it's immediately noticeable. And over time, noticeable conveniences add up in a customer's mind, as do noticeable hassles and shortcomings and service charges. If a customer starts complaining about a few of these, very soon a friend will say, "Why don't you move your accounts to Bank X?" Or an ad on a screen will say it, and the customer is gone.

The bottom line applies not only to banks but also to businesses of many kinds. A company that grows bigger strategically—using IT power in combination with smart management moves, as Friendly is doing—gets more chances to attract and retain customers and sell more to them.

Hidden Benefits and Key Takeaways

There's more. Good things (as well as bad things) happen behind the scenes, where customers never see them, but the company feels the impacts. We have looked at existing IT systems in many smaller to midsized companies, including standalone regional banks. Where are the servers? Often in a closet, literally, with a backup generator in the basement in case the power goes out. Most of the time that's fine. It may not be fine if the area should have a flood, a fire, or who knows what.

Servers today belong in the cloud. AWS is a common choice; private clouds are available too. Bigger banks with more IT savvy and spending power, like Friendly Bank, generally can provide more security behind the scenes.

Centralized integration of systems also pays off in ways that customers don't see. Do you enjoy software updates? They're constantly coming wherever there is software. On your personal phone or home computer they are mostly painless, though sometimes not. On sizable business systems, they can be a recurring pain in the overhead. The job is especially onerous if a lot of updates, new additions, and security patches have to be installed and checked separately at separate offices. With unified systems in the cloud, you update once and everyone everywhere is ready to roll. The people at Friendly Bank do it that way … with a little help from their friendly IT contractors.

Other hidden benefits can be described but they get very technical. We will spare you the details. The important takeaways are these:

- Information technology changes everything about every business. And it keeps on changing things.

- In such an environment, there is no safe harbor within which you can bunker down. Smart companies go out to ride the waves. *You must thrive to survive.*

- This requires strategic thinking. Information technology is not a substitute for business sense, nor is it a substitute for sound execution.

- IT is, however, a necessary weapon for every strategic business move. When you're in the IT-verse—as we all are nowadays— you thrive by using the coin of the realm.

Acting on these key points will take you a long way. Further informed, we hope, by the story that comes next.

CHAPTER 4:

Finding a Blue Ocean and Founding a Business Powered by IT

H istory repeats itself. The patterns are similar; only the forms are new. So let us frame the story of Mr. X, a modern energy entrepreneur, with a whirlwind recap of the history of American energy industries.

For centuries these industries have been at the hub of the nation's growth. The ongoing search for better sources of power and fuel has always been driven by entrepreneurs combining new technologies with new business strategies. And repeatedly, the quest for the next winning formula leaves some players in the dust while others flourish.

The quest for the next winning formula leaves some players in the dust while others flourish.

A Brief History of Energy—from Whaling to Deregulation

During the early 1800s, sea captains like the fictional Captain Ahab in *Moby-Dick* used the latest navigation methods to sail far from home in pursuit of a hot commodity. Whale oil was the preferred fuel for lamps and lighting. But this brutal business model grew unsustainable, as demand literally began to kill off the supply. The whales were saved when rising prices spurred innovation in producing kerosene and other fossil-based fuels.

In 1859, in a rural corner of Pennsylvania, an inexperienced well-driller had a simple but brilliant idea. Edwin Drake was part of a startup company with a novel mission: drilling for petroleum in large quantities. Traces of the gooey liquid were seeping to the surface along a stream called Oil Creek. Could big reserves lie deep underground? Local folks laughed at the seemingly hopeless project. Whenever Drake's crew drilled below a certain depth, the walls of the borehole kept collapsing. His simple solution was driving lengths of iron pipe down into the hole to reinforce it. Drilling resumed, and at 69.5 feet, America's first great oil boom began.

Drake himself didn't prosper. He had not secured rights to nearby land, so competitors came swarming in. Nor did he file for patents on the "drivepipe" approach, which was used everywhere—including at Spindle-top in Texas, decades later, setting off that state's even bigger oil boom.

Meanwhile, inventor-entrepreneurs in the Northeast focused on harnessing electricity. In the late 1800s, Thomas Edison and George Westinghouse waged their famous "war of currents" to determine whether the country's future electric grids would run on direct or alternating current. Edison moved first. Deploying proven technology, he built numerous small, neighborhood-sized distribution systems powered by local DC generators. Westinghouse overtook him with a second-mover leapfrog strategy. He acquired and developed newer AC technologies that were much more scalable because AC could be transmitted over long distances. Edison lost the tech battle and also lost control of his electrical company when financiers merged it with another to form General Electric.

From the early to mid-1900s, the energy industries were consolidated and simplified. Utility companies across the nation, from Central Maine Power to California's Pacific Gas and Electric, delivered electricity and/or natural gas to customers in their respective market areas. Each enjoyed near-monopoly status in exchange for public regulation, while a few big petroleum companies provided most of the fuels for motor vehicles, ships, and planes. But the picture was never really that simple. Countless companies of all kinds and sizes fought for a host of niches: as equipment makers and contractors, exploration firms, securities underwriters, and more.

Then, in the 1990s, came deregulation. Since both electricity and gas can be sent over long distances, many states started allowing customers to buy energy from a choice of providers, in which case their local utilities would serve only for last-mile distribution. Today, about half of the states in the United States have deregulated markets. And a new breed of middleman firms has sprung up: retail energy companies.

The retail companies are asset light. They don't generate or drill. Rather, they buy energy contracts from myriad sources, then bundle and resell the energy to end users. It's a complicated business, riddled with cost and risk, and highly competitive.

Out of this milieu came Mr. X. He had a Blue-Ocean vision for a new kind of energy company that could take root and grow, separate from the crush. It would be sustainable and scalable, built for future energy markets as well as today's, and it would be built on a flexible platform from another industry: information technology.

Setting the Parameters for an IT-Based Energy Startup

We met Mr. X in 2008 when he was vice president of a major energy retailer. A few years later, when he launched his own company, he became our personal client. We helped him execute the IT aspects of his vision, which went as follows.

He wanted to stay away from the retail model of selling directly to users. That would require hefty ongoing expenses for marketing and sales. Also, if you were to sell to residential customers along with businesses, as most energy retailers do, you would probably need separate ad campaigns and sales teams for the different markets.

Mr. X's goal was to hone down the business model, minimizing costs on every line of EBITDA while targeting his efforts to achieve high, recurring revenues. Such revenues could best be found in the commercial/institutional market. These users buy energy in bulk, not just in household amounts … and many buy their energy through brokers.

Under deregulation, purchasing electricity or natural gas becomes a complex matter in its own right. The energy can be bought at a fixed rate for, say, twelve months, or at a variable rate that goes down (or up) as market conditions change. Blended contracts can also be had, pricing some portion of energy use at a fixed rate and some variably. Users committed to going green often want green contracts, with at least such-and-such percent of their electricity from renewable sources. Therefore, businesses that don't have the staff or the inclination to sift through all the possible ways of getting a good price will count on a specialist—a broker—to do it for them.

Mr. X intended his new company to serve the brokers. He knew they weren't being served as well as they could be by the retail companies. A broker would ask for a quote on behalf of a client, spelling out to a sales rep the volume of energy and the contract terms that he was looking for. The retailer's rep then had to search and compare offers from various energy suppliers in order to put together a best-price quote. Often it might take three to five days for the rep to get back to the broker. If the broker's client then wanted to see a different set of quotes on different contract terms, the search-and-wait loop began all over again.

Here, Mr. X reasoned, was a process that begged for digitization. A searchable database of products and prices, regularly updated, should allow quotes to be turned around faster by a much leaner staff. Brokers who partnered with his company could log onto the platform to get rapid, reliable service every time. In short, Mr. X was thinking the way Jeff Bezos did for the launch of Amazon. He thought in terms of building *an IT company to provide services,* instead of a business firm that would use some IT.

This mindset enabled him to think of other services that could be offered to brokers on an IT platform. For example, some brokers sometimes like to take their commissions out of the front end of a big sale—maybe to splurge on a new Escalade or a vacation—while some prefer payments month by month. Surely, features to handle these desires could be built in. And nearly all energy brokers, being independent operators of limited size, had concerns about monitoring their cash flow. Features to help with that could be built in too. Mr. X wanted brokers to think of his company's platform as their second cyber-home. The more they did so, the stickier the platform would become, giving the company repeat business from loyal broker-partners with minimal outbound marketing.

The startup concept looked solid all around. All that remained was to do it.

Implementing the Vision: How an Ambitious IT Project Was Done Right

To avoid the hassles of launching from scratch, Mr. X bought an existing energy company of moderate size. YZ Energy (as we're calling it here) would gradually be converted to run as he envisioned. Our firm helped with the project, augmenting the work done by YZ Energy's internal IT staff. And what impressed us throughout was the brilliance with which Mr. X led the entire process.

As noted in chapter 1, most major business IT projects fail to meet their goals. This one succeeded because the CEO set the proper conditions for success. Here are several key moves that Mr. X made, which in our judgment helped significantly.

HE URGED HIS PEOPLE TO CONCENTRATE ON THE VISION, NOT ON "THE PLAN." As an experienced executive, he knew that in complex projects of any kind, unforeseen things will happen. And while advance planning is certainly needed, it's all too easy for our methodical human minds to get stuck in the details of the plan. We may overreact or overcompensate when a particular sequence of steps doesn't go as planned; we may spend so much time hugging trees that we get lost in the forest.

While advance planning is certainly needed, it's all too easy for our methodical human minds to get stuck in the details of the plan.

Therefore, Mr. X emphasized keeping the broader vision in view. The basic mindset that he encouraged could be described as follows: "We're on a journey to become a company that looks like *this* [i.e., the vision]. So, given where we are now, what do we need to do next?"

HE MADE THE PROJECT A TRUE COLLABORATION. As the new CEO of YZ Energy, Mr. X gathered his business leaders—the CFO; the heads of sales, products, and operations—together with the IT leader. After ensuring that the vision was crystal clear to everyone, he made it equally clear that everyone would be working together on it. YZ was to be recreated as a platform company, and the business and IT teams would form a unified team of cocreators, interacting and exchanging information continually from day one forward.

The approach was a fundamental departure from the way that big IT projects typically are tackled. How it's usually done goes something like this: the businesspeople come up with an idea and outline it to the IT department. From the information they've been given, the IT people create a requirements document—which may take a few months—and they present it to business leadership for signoff. Then the IT people hunker down in their own domain, working on the software until it's ready to be handed over to the business side for testing and bug reporting.

Such a process may seem collaborative since back-and-forth exchanges are involved. But in between the backs and the forths, most creation takes place in isolation. Which leaves too much room for the separate teams to go off on diverging tangents. Mr. X did not want that to occur, so he forged a more complete collaboration and ensured that the following step was taken as well.

THE PROJECT'S "BIG VISION" WAS BROKEN OUT INTO ACHIEVABLE QUARTERLY GOALS. "Divide and conquer" is a classic strategy for attacking any complex task. Often, it is understood to mean breaking out the puzzle into solvable pieces, but the principle also applies along the dimension of time. On a complex journey, you don't want to march for too long between compass checks or you may wander far into the wilderness.

Mr. X had the project set up so that the team could win fast or fail fast on each leg of the journey. The business and IT people settled into a nice cadence of working together toward quarterly milestones. And since not every quarter's work was totally successful, the frequent checking allowed them to see in a timely fashion if anything was going wrong. Sometimes, for example, they found a key portion of the project heading in a direction that the market was unlikely to support. Then they were able to pivot quickly and reestablish a better course.

Throughout the process, Mr. X preached a mantra that went approximately as follows: "Yes, we have a big vision, but we don't need to start a revolution. Instead, let's have a series of evolutions that will revolutionize the industry."

THE CEO AND HIS LEADERSHIP TEAM UNDERSTOOD THAT IT SPENDING WOULD HAVE TO BE HIGHER THAN USUAL THROUGH-OUT THE PROJECT. Under normal circumstances, most companies benchmark their relative IT spend against an industry average. If they are spending a much higher percentage of revenues than their peers, leadership will probably decide that IT budget-cutting is in order. But if you are transforming a conventional energy company into a new kind of IT platform company, those are not normal circumstances.

Mr. X was willing to invest heavily in IT up front—and to maintain a high level of investment through completion of the project—because he foresaw, correctly, that the end product would give his company a *sustainable competitive advantage*. YZ Energy would be able to offer a desirable suite of services that would be new and unique to the industry. Moreover, the net financial result would be to produce growing, recurring revenues at lower-than-usual operating costs, which translates to a better bottom line in EBITDA. In short, the math said to spend, so he did. If he had not committed to this crucial decision for the lifetime of the transformation project, YZ Energy could never have succeeded to the extent that it has. And finally:

THE CONCEPT OF BREAKING THE PROJECT INTO MANAGEABLE CHUNKS WAS APPLIED TO THE FINAL GO-TO-MARKET STAGES, INCLUDING ROLLOUT OF THE PLATFORM AND EXPANSION INTO NEW MARKETS. You're probably familiar with the Lean Startup methodology.[3] Among other things, it suggests testing your market initially with a minimum viable product: one that has enough basic functionality to make people want to pay for it and use it but doesn't yet include all the bells and whistles you envision. The idea is actually not so new. It simply means offering people something of value, from which you can get a return, and then adding more value in stages. That way, further product development can go hand in hand with market rollout. The whole venture becomes an iterative learning process, which, if done well, should lead to optimum results with minimal wasted investment.

And that is essentially how YZ Energy proceeded with its broker platform.

Outcomes and Benefits: How a Good Idea Grew

The platform's most basic function was to automate (and speed up) the process of giving brokers price quotations on energy packages that they could purchase for their clients. The platform went to market, initially, with some but not all of that functionality. At first it only produced automated quotes for fixed-rate energy purchases. Variable-rate and combined-rate quotes were added shortly afterward.

---

3   If not, see Eric Ries, *The Lean Startup: How Today's Entrepreneurs Use Continuous Innovation to Create Radically Successful Businesses* (New York: Crown Business, 2011).

Performance met expectations. Brokers who formerly had to wait days for each round of quotes could now get multiple quotes within the same day. Their clients, the end users, were pleased. As the word spread, more brokers joined without YZ Energy needing to do any marketing outreach whatsoever.

Over a period of a year or so, more features and functions were added. A key one was the feature that allowed brokers to choose how they would take their commission. Then came some truly sophisticated stuff, such as giving brokers the ability to analyze their clients' patterns of energy use. Eventually, brokers were finding that they could *run their entire business* from the YZ Energy platform. It indeed became their new home in cyberspace: a platform as sticky as one could possibly want.

Concurrently, expansion into new geographic markets proceeded in stages too. After initial rollout in a large southern state, gradually YZ Energy picked up brokers serving energy-deregulated states throughout the United States. Then it expanded into several Canadian provinces. Along the way, this growth attracted investors who purchased YZ Energy not to strip its assets, but to keep it going. And better yet …

Because Mr. X had done such a fine job of controlling expenses while maximizing revenue, YZ Energy merited a nice acquisition price. It was sold for about *three times more* than the valuation of conventional retail energy companies of similar size.

At present, under new ownership, YZ Energy is still growing. Global expansion might well be in its future. For a company that started at only moderate size with a conventional business model, the story is remarkable. It is a testament to the power of entrepreneurial thinking combined with the inherent leverage of IT in one of the world's most crucial and fast-evolving industries.

CHAPTER 5:

Reinventing a Sales Model with IT and AI

There are many ways a business can fall behind the curve and get in trouble. Usually, we think of companies failing to adapt to new technologies, with Blockbuster Video being a sort of poster child for the issue. But that is not the only source from which potentially fatal problems can arise. In some cases, a company has a core business practice that threatens to drive the bottom line into the red. In those cases, technology often becomes part of the solution.

Here is a story that makes the point. As usual, the company's name has been changed, but the facts are real.

An Insecure Way to Sell Security?

Lenox Security provides home security systems. You may have such a system, which you activate when you go to sleep or are away from the house. The basic setup includes sensors on doorframes and window frames to detect whether one of these points of entry is being opened. Should a bad actor try coming in, the system sets off a noisy alarm while alerting the local police. Customers can also buy many enhancements to the basics—motion detectors, security cameras, smoke and flood detectors—and the security aspects can be integrated with smart-home technology that does things like regulating temperatures.

Home security has been a growth market across the United States for decades. At the time we began working with the company, Lenox had been riding that wave, showing consistent top-line revenue growth year after year. But one big problem loomed ahead. The costs of acquiring customers were rising at a faster rate than revenues.

That's an ominous sign. Simple math says that when the cost of delivering something to market approaches or exceeds the money you can earn from it, you are in trouble. Often this occurs in markets where a once-profitable product becomes a commodity, driving down the prices that a maker can charge. In the early 2000s, IBM exited the personal computer market for this reason, selling its PC business to a Chinese firm, while Kodak ran into trouble by coming late to the digital camera market. Given the spending required to make its cameras match the competition for features and functions, Kodak lost money on every unit sold.

The situation at Lenox Security was different. Although there was certainly competition, including price competition, around every item from system components to installation and service, the cost category that threatened profits did not lie anywhere in the supply chain. Nor did it lie in manufacturing, or in operating costs, or in any such item that typically goes into the cost of goods sold. The ticking time bomb lay in the cost of *selling*—in the sales model that was key to the company's overall business model.

Nearly all of Lenox's sales came through a single channel: its nationwide network of local dealers. Most of the dealers were (and are) independent, entrepreneurial salespeople. Some had backgrounds in security (e.g., retired police officers). Others brought experience and contacts they'd gained in various residential service industries, and more than a few had built their own regional sales teams. Under a typical "partner" arrangement, dealers of these types earn commissions from Lenox by prospecting for leads, selling systems, and getting customers to renew their service contracts. Lenox would then handle everything else, as needed, from system installation to 24/7 security monitoring of the homes under contract.

The company incurred (and still incurs) ongoing costs to maintain a dealer/partner network. In order to have a suitable presence in metro areas throughout the country, Lenox must often recruit and train new dealers. Then come the costs of paying commissions and managing dealer relationships. Furthermore, at the time of our contact with Lenox, another cost element was starting to look particularly ominous.

Lenox was using a growth strategy that consisted of "buying out" selected dealers. Picture a dealer who has ten thousand homes under contract in a prime metro area. Lenox might propose an offer to that dealer, as follows: *Look, we'd like to buy these customers from you outright. We'll pay a price equal to the earnings you would get from them over the next X months.* For the dealer involved, the offer may be very attractive. It's like an exit strategy for an investor. The dealer can be done with those ten thousand customers, reap a sizable profit, and move on to finding another ten thousand, who can also be sold.

Meanwhile, Lenox gains some advantages too. The company avoids the ongoing costs of commissions and such while bringing a big batch of good customers under its direct control. But now consider a major downside. With each buyout, the company was running ahead of itself in terms of cash flow. So Lenox made leveraged buyouts, incurring debt in order to grow. Eventually, the debt and interest on the debt were, as mentioned, growing faster than top-line revenue. This trend was unsustainable. The model behind it needed to be rethought. That was why the company's leaders called us in for help with a new plan they had devised.

Going Direct

While local dealers would remain part of Lenox for the foreseeable future, they could no longer be counted on as the sole foundation and fulcrum of sales. Lenox wanted to open up new channels, selling directly to customers. Moreover, top management intended to do this without investing in bricks and mortar or creating an extensive in-house sales staff. The goal was to keep growing the top line while minimizing the total cost of marketing, sales, and customer retention. And how was all of the above to be accomplished? By leveraging information technology.

Together with the Lenox management team, we worked out a multilayered approach. Marketing and sales to new prospects—along with upselling to, and retention of, existing customers—would be migrated gradually to multiple digital channels. The Lenox website would be redesigned. Social media, digital ads, mobile communications, SMS, email, and more would come into play. Each would be used wherever and whenever it promised to be most effective.

The whole package added up to a massive, complex undertaking. Like other digitization projects that we've described in previous chapters, it had to be implemented gradually, in a series of actionable steps. In many respects it would make sense to start by going after low-hanging fruit, and then moving up the tree. But, in concert with such a gradual start, we'd have to take a series of foundational steps as well.

This project entailed communicating directly with individual customers and prospects—millions of them. In order to be effective, getting high rates of return on digital outreach, Lenox couldn't simply throw a lot of messaging into cyberspace and hope that some of it hit home. The likely outcome would be lots of people seeing Lenox as a digital pest, of which there are many, while large numbers of prospective buyers might be overlooked or might not receive the kind of messaging that speaks to them. For best results, the digital direct campaigns had to be targeted as precisely as possible, which could be done by using new tools to explore and exploit a vast existing resource.

Data and the Mining Thereof

The existing resource, of course, is customer data. Everyone who uses any form of digital media leaves a long and growing trail of data about themselves. Your IP address shows where you live. The calls and texts you make with your mobile phone show where you go. Everything you buy with a card or a mobile app creates data about your purchasing patterns. The websites you visit reveal your interests; your social media use reveals that and more. Any company can gain access to much of this data about a sea of potential prospects. And nearly every company has an even richer pool of data about its existing customers.

Lenox Security, being widely established, had immense amounts of data about legions of homeowners, landlords, and tenants who were already using its systems. That was the good news. These existing customers were the low-hanging fruit. In general, retaining customers is much less costly than finding and bringing in new ones. If we could market to them effectively, inducing them to renew or upgrade their service—or to refer people they know as new customers—the payback from those efforts alone should be significant. And Lenox's customer data would be the guide to targeting the efforts.

The bad news: different forms of customer data were scattered across different systems within the company. Basic nuts-and-bolts data resided on islands in the billing system, installation records, security-monitoring logs, and so forth. Phone calls to the automated service number were recorded in interactive voice response. Online chats and data from the dealers could be helpful, too, but they also resided elsewhere.

By combing through all of the disaggregated data and by looking for meaningful correlations, we hoped to be able to fine-tune our marketing messages *as well as the optimum channels to use.* For example, we might deduce that Joe Jones in Boston is likely to renew if he's offered a fixed-rate contract for the next three years, whereas Maria Lopez in Phoenix would be more motivated by a smart thermostat to control her whole-house air conditioning. We might also find that Joe responds to emails, but Maria operates by text, while certain customers in L.A. are best reached by prompts in their mobile apps, and certain neighbors of theirs respond best when they are pinged through a combination of channels. These sorts of findings would be the ideal.

How to attain the ideal was the challenge. Some companies hire teams of analysts to mine their data. The analysts are smart. They're armed with software tools that work well for comparing and correlating data between datasets—provided the analysts know which datasets to search. And provided they are capable of hunting everywhere so as not to miss anything. The trouble is that meaningful data may indeed be found in many places, and if the data on each customer comprises, say, hundreds of data points and touchpoints distributed through every system the company owns, no team of humans can ever find and analyze all the possible connections. They're limited to fishing in just a few parts of the lake.

At the other end of the spectrum, companies can buy ready-made data analyses from providers like Nielsen. A Nielsen marketing report can be applied to both your prospects and your existing customers. The shortcoming here is that the information clumps people into demographic groups. It may tell you, for instance, how millennials or midwestern married couples tend to behave when it comes to buying preferences and responses to digital marketing. But are all millennials alike? Hardly. Likewise, people in the same income bracket or the same political party do not necessarily act the same in how they spend their money and their digital attention spans. So you're left with general guidance that may often be useful to an extent, or maybe not.

Today, with advances in IT, even moderate-sized companies can do better than either of the two options just described. Artificial intelligence has developed to the point of being affordable for strategic business use. Smart AI agents can plow through mountains of data, leaving no stones unturned, initially, by virtue of their sheer data-crunching capacity. These agents can also "learn" as they go, refining their searches to home in on linkages that look statistically significant.

> **Artificial intelligence has developed to the point of being affordable for strategic business use.**

Those are the kinds of tools we've been applying with Lenox. We find that by using intelligent AI intelligently, we can often drill right down to the ideal level of individualized, person-by-person analysis. Lenox therefore gains a *deep understanding* of its customers, an understanding that can be augmented and leveraged repeatedly in many marketing efforts to come.

Results to Date

As we write this chapter, Lenox is about three years into its digital transition. Local dealers still play a major role in sales growth and will continue to play an important role. But digital direct marketing is taking on an increasing portion of the work and is doing the job effectively.

- At the start of the project, customer attrition was 17 percent per year. The last time we checked, it was under 9 percent. This reduction in attrition (or increase in retention, however you want to put it) is driving around a million dollars of additional EBITDA per quarter.

- When the project began, direct-to-customer channels produced only 4 percent of total sales. These channels now produce over 21 percent while contributing to sustained top-line revenue growth *without* a corresponding greater growth in debt load.

In short, Lenox is moving in the right direction. It is also moving ahead of rivals that do not use IT or AI in similarly powerful ways. The Lenox Security story illustrates several key takeaways we would like to leave you with:

Now that every company is an IT company, a new IT approach is almost always a key part of the solution.

- Existential threats to a company's bottom line do not always come from external market pressures. Some threats can arise internally, through use of a business model or sales model that's unsustainable.

- It helps greatly if management can notice the unsustainable trend and take action to change it before the effects become toxic. Change is difficult. Last-minute rescues tend more to the category of "impossible."

- Now that every company is an IT company, a new IT approach is almost always a key part of the solution.

- Major projects must be broken into manageable, measurable stages. Start by doing what is essential and will deliver value. Then add and build from there.

- In a project that involves changing how you sell, don't shortchange the fundamental steps of understanding your customers and prospects as thoroughly as you can. Today's IT tools, including AI, can give you a solid platform for launching the company into new levels of sales performance.

CHAPTER 6:

Boosting Returns from Embedded Technology in Manufacturing

M anufacturing all over the world, including in the United States, continues to remain a crucial part of the economy. The manufacturing sector has always been at the cutting edge of technology. It is a business that requires using the best, latest tools and techniques to make goods that are the latest and best. Further, these goods must be produced at the lowest possible cost in order to reap profits that keep the enterprise alive. A key enabler for meeting this challenge is having the ability to set up, control, and reconfigure the manufacturing equipment at every step of the process, as well as for the whole production line—while also monitoring data about production quality.

In recent years the ability to do all these things has been enhanced tremendously by digital technology. A state-of-the-art manufacturing operation today isn't just highly automated; it is intelligent. Embedded sensors and microcontrollers make the machines precise and adaptive. If you're turning out multiple versions of a product, the machinery can be programmed to switch from one task to a similar but different task in a flash. And in today's world—where key people and facilities are spatially distributed but interconnected—it is essential to be able to monitor and control the entire process via the internet.

Getting to this happy state has not been easy. Our firm, CG Infinity, actually had its roots in helping manufacturers move into the digital age. And why would they need such assistance? Because while manufacturing firms may have technical expertise that is far beyond that of the typical banker or merchant, they're often on unfamiliar turf when they venture deep into the realm of chips and software. They are used to working with atoms (physical materials), whereas getting electrons to behave is another kind of game.

We'll share a story of how we worked with one company to solve a few tricky problems. The problems were quite different in nature, but they had a common theme: the need to *control* what's going on. And, as in some previous chapters, let's begin by putting this modern-day quest for control into historical context.

Today's issues become clearer once we see them reflected throughout the history of mass-production manufacturing. If you have studied that history, you may know of an enterprise that flourished on the east coast of Italy centuries ago.

People Power in Action; New Dimensions of Complexity

From late medieval times into the Renaissance, the Republic of Venice ruled the waves in the Mediterranean and beyond. The Venetians floated thousands of high-quality merchant ships and war galleys, turning them out with amazing speed in a shipbuilding and armaments plant that's considered one of the first mass-production factories. In the early 1500s, the Arsenal of Venice[4] covered sixty waterfront acres and employed about sixteen thousand. The Arsenal used highly stratified divisions of labor and precise specifications for interchangeable parts. There were elaborate systems for managing supply chains, inventory, and quality control. The Arsenal even had a moving assembly line. As soon as carpenters and caulkers finished the wooden hull and deck of a ship, it could be floated along a canal past stations where the iron-workers were ready with anchors, guns, and fittings; the sailmakers and rope-makers then added their components, and so on. Near the end, bakers put biscuits aboard for the crew.

Mass production on this level wouldn't be widely replicated elsewhere for centuries to come. Then again, the Venetians had spent centuries building up and refining the Arsenal to the state described here. This had required massive, sustained investment, funded largely by the returns from sea-trading. And above all, it required vast human resources.

Much has been made of the fact that in early manufacturing, nearly everything had to be done by hand—that is, by humans. What's often missed is that everything also had to be controlled by humans. The Arsenal of Venice relied on craft guilds and apprenticeships to

---

4   A wealth of research on the Arsenal of Venice has been published, much of it in Italian. One good source in English is Frederic Chapin Lane's *Venetian Ships and Shipbuilders of the Renaissance* (Baltimore: Johns Hopkins University Press, 1992).

teach people how to do things and to monitor their skills. Small armies of accountants and managers tracked and coordinated every aspect of production. Then and for years afterward, even as the factory system gradually spread to other industries, all processes relied not only on human labor, but also on constant human attention.

That began to change in the late 1700s when the Industrial Revolution was triggered by James Watt's steam engine, along with automated production equipment like the power loom. But while these inventions reduced the need for human input, they added layers of complexity in terms of technology and control.

Meeting the challenges took a long time. The first few generations of steam engines were tragically prone to explode. Other machinery needed speed governors and automatic braking or cutoff systems. Keeping the output within tolerances so that parts fit together was a task in itself, especially since making just about anything, from shoes to railroad cars, still involved a lot of handwork. (It's said that the development of machine tools during the 1800s was a matter of "embedding skills in the tools instead of in people.") Moreover, all the tools and controls had to be mechanical until electricity was mastered years later.

Truly modern mass production arrived in the 1900s. By mid-century, at least in industrialized countries like the United States, most families could afford electric refrigerators that self-regulated the temperature inside. These mass-market marvels were put together in factories using "Fordist" production techniques—named after Henry Ford, whose company deployed arrays of electromechanical systems to build even more complex products, automobiles, in high volumes efficiently.

But production lines of that era had their limits. Despite efficiency gains, they generated tons of mismade scrap. Also, once a line was hardwired and bolted in place to make a standardized product, it couldn't be reconfigured easily to make different versions. Better approaches came from two directions. One was Japan, where manufacturers like Toyota[5] combined shop-floor redesign with human use of new process control methods to reduce waste and achieve flexibility.

The other source of advance has been computing. Since our firm is headed by people who've been a close part of this movement, the sections ahead are drawn mostly from firsthand experience.

Where Intelligence Lives

Early computers, the big mainframe models, had nothing to do with real-time manufacturing control. Born for military and counterespionage use, they first found their way into business as number-crunching aids for record-keeping and planning. Then came miniaturization. After tiny transistors replaced bulky vacuum tubes, integrated circuits made it possible to have a computer on a chip—or at least, processing power on a chip. You could then write software that ran on chunks of hardware about the size of a postage stamp. (As indeed our founder, Bhopi Dhall, did from the 1970s onward.)

This has been more than an evolutionary step. It is proving to be revolutionary. In much the same way that nineteenth-century technology embedded skills in machine tools, modern computing technology embeds intelligence, both in manufacturing plants and in their output. It's now common to see production lines that can think and act for themselves to a large degree, turning out products that do the same.

The embedded-intelligence revolution affects the makers of almost all physical products, from cars to processed foods. They've

---

5   The chief architect of Toyota's approach was industrial engineer Taiichi Ohno. See his book
     Toyota Production System (Boca Raton, FL: CRC Press, 1988).

been having to rethink how they do almost everything, and the need is urgent because the scope and uses of embedded intelligence are increasing rapidly. Consider how the pace of change has ramped up in motor vehicles. From the early 1900s into the 1970s, most cars had only rudimentary self-governing mechanisms under the hood. Outside the powertrain, they typically had only two features that actuated automatically: the brake lights, which lit up when you hit the brake pedal, and the little interior light that clicked on when you opened the door.

Contrast that with what is available today. Completely self-driving vehicles aren't yet safe for everyday use, but they exist. And even moderately priced cars carry an astounding load of IT systems for functions that range from fuel economy to driver-assist safety features to a Wi-Fi hotspot. When General Motors rolled out its 2019 Chevrolet Volt, the hybrid was written up not only in *Car and Driver* but also in *Wired*. According to the latter, the Volt had "over 100 electronic controllers," with onboard systems running a total of ten million lines of software code—more than the Boeing 787 airliner.[6]

Uncertainties Ahead: The Manufacturer's Dilemma

The 2019 Volt is already history as we write this. So are some notorious flops like the Juicero, the Wi-Fi-enabled kitchen appliance that was meant to revolutionize juice making. Instead, the Juicero turned into a poster child for technology overkill, a danger every manufacturer should try to avoid. If you use digital tech to do what doesn't really need doing or could easily be done in a simpler way, all you are likely

---

6   Jason Paur, "Chevy Volt: King of (Software) Cars," *Wired*, November 5, 2018, https://www.wired.com/2010/11/chevy-volt-king-of-software-cars/.

to accomplish is adding cost without value. IT should always be applied in ways that will impact EBITDA positively.

This can be tricky, since digital technology is still relatively young, and the embedded kind is younger still. There are bound to be applications that misfire. The fact to keep in mind is that embedded, distributed, and networked intelligence is racing forward, nonetheless. Almost everyone you meet is either carrying some or wearing it. Almost every modern physical space you enter—whether it is a fixed space, like a building, or a moving space, like a vehicle—is monitored or controlled to some degree by digital systems.

IT should always be applied in ways that will impact EBITDA positively.

What all of this will lead to over the next few years is uncertain. Maybe the fulfillment of some current vision of the Internet of Things, or maybe entirely different scenarios. The trick is using human intelligence (the original kind) to conduct your own digital innovation strategically.

And as we've said, this is difficult for many manufacturers, including many of the best. Problems often arise from the silo effect, which was pointed out in chapter 2 and elsewhere. Most companies tend to have their IT-related function(s) separated from functions on the business side, and organizational isolation is only part of the issue. There are gaps between how the two sides think, speak, and operate, which stem from underlying gaps in their areas of expertise and focus.

Chapters 7 and 8 will get into recommendations for bridging these gaps. For now, let's keep our eye on the manufacturing sector, and let's admit that some manufacturers do not have to worry much about integrating digital technology into their operations or product designs. Companies like Intel and Apple were digital natives from day one. But for many others, despite their mechanical sophistication or their knowledge of materials or chemical processes, modern digital sensing and control is a moving target.

It's tough for them to keep up with advances in the field, and their in-house capabilities are finite. So they often hire contractors to help with the design work, as GM did by asking IBM to help with the Volt.[7] The need is often greatest among specialty or midsized manufacturers, which are essential to our economy but may have limited abilities to stay at the cutting edge of embedded intelligence.

Here is a story from our work with one client.

How an Industry Leader Kept Its Leading Edge

The fictional name of this real manufacturer is The Joiner Company. Its core products are automated welding systems, and Joiner is known for making top-notch equipment. The product line is extensive. Joiner's machines apply several different welding and joining techniques to bond plastics, metals, and sometimes other materials, creating sturdy seams that don't require fasteners or adhesives.

Customers also span a wide range. Automakers and their suppliers choose systems from the Joiner lineup for attaching bumper assemblies, welding engine parts or mufflers together, and more. Food processors use Joiner equipment to seal plastic packaging. Other systems are used for making items from baby diapers to medical instruments.

In short, Joiner is a manufacturer's manufacturer. And the company has been among the industry's best in building smart systems

---

7   IBM played a key role in the design of the 2011 Volt, the car's first model year. GM then carried many of IBM's features and design approaches into subsequent Volt models. See, for example, Rick Merritt, "IBM Tells Story behind Chevy Volt Design," *EE Times*, May 4, 2011, https://www. eetimes.com/ibm-tells-story-behind-chevy-volt-design/.

with electronics and software that make the machines highly programmable and adaptable. From 1999 into the 2000s, they called on us several times for aid with a variety of issues, including four big ones.

CONTROLLING THE FORCE—This was a software problem at the very point of application. The machine in question was an ultrasonic vibration welder, which can join two plastic parts as follows: while one part is held in place, the machine brings the other down in contact with it. An ultrasonic burst induces high-frequency vibrations in the area where they touch, heating the plastic until it melts just enough for the parts to fuse. Once the weld has set, the assembly is lifted out and two more parts are loaded in.

The entire sequence happens without human intervention, and it happens *fast*. The machine is capable of sixty to seventy welds per minute, which means a second or less for each cycle. Engineers at Joiner had software on a chip to control nearly all of the variables—the distance of travel to bring the parts together, the intensity of the ultrasonic burst, the timing of the sequence—and to adjust these variables if the machine had to switch to welding different kinds of parts.

What eluded them was writing an algorithm to control one key variable: the contact force that the machine exerted on the parts. The touch had to be just right for the vibration heating and welding to occur. And then a different level of force was needed to hold the parts together while the semi-molten plastic cooled and hardened to firm up the weld. Of course, the Joiner engineers understood how the machine worked physically. Contact force was driven by a compressed-air piston. To vary the force, you tweaked the pressure valve. The engineers just couldn't translate their understanding to lines of code that would do the job in the manner desired.

Bhopi, our founder, tackled this one for Joiner. His fundamental knowledge of physics, combined with deep expertise in software, enabled him to write the code that assured The Force would be with the machine's users.

GETTING PAID FOR CAPABILITIES USED—Joiner sold each machine at a range of price points, depending on whether the client wanted basic control functionality or additional features for more advanced forms of control. Clients in a certain overseas markets were buying at entry-level prices. They received machines with fully loaded software packages but with the premium features shut off. It wasn't hard to learn how to unlock those features. The clients enjoyed deluxe performance at a nice discount while depriving Joiner of rightful revenue.

The solution had to defeat the practice and keep it from spreading. We took an approach that was novel at the time in the early 2000s, though it's common today. Every machine shipped by Joiner was set up to be linked over the internet to Joiner HQ. The machines' control systems could then be activated remotely, and activation of any and all features was linked to the accounting department. From that point forward, people had to pay for what they used, leading to significant top-line gains for Joiner.

SAFETY CERTIFICATION—Clients in the European Union want machinery with the Union's "CE" mark of safety approval. To earn the CE, Joiner had to demonstrate that workers would be reasonably protected from being injured by its welding machines, even if they were to make the kinds of mistakes or missteps that are characteristic of our human race. This entailed some reworking of the control systems, with which we helped. For example, the function that sets the machine in motion was software separated from all other functions to minimize the risk of triggering it by accident.

A COMMON ARCHITECTURE—Linking the machines by internet, as described above, did more than force free riders to pay the correct fare. It was part of a series of steps that eventually led to major savings in design, manufacturing, and operating costs for Joiner. Without going too far into technical details, here in a nutshell is what we helped the company to do.

Since Joiner makes a variety of machines that use different welding technologies for different purposes, unifying the control systems became a concern. Custom-designing the microprocessors and software for each machine would be a nightmare to begin with. It would also create ongoing hassles with interfaces and integration when installing the machines to work in a complex factory environment.

What we developed for Joiner was a common-controller architecture. It exploits the capabilities of a powerful chip of a single kind, which can be embedded in any of the machines with minimal customization needed. Also, most of the customization can be done in software, which is cheaper to make and easier to change than hardware. Meanwhile, internet connection enables many conveniences. Joiner service reps can troubleshoot a client's system remotely; a client with multiple assembly plants can monitor and control them from one point, and so forth.

Much of what we did with Joiner is now standard practice. Much of it no longer needs to be done from scratch, either. Just as construction electricians can now install premade modules in buildings to replace the need for a lot of on-site wiring, modular solutions are available in the world of embedded control. Technology keeps changing perpetually. When our firm works with manufacturers these days, it's usually in the areas of business IT systems and integrating those systems with intelligent process control. But there is still plenty to be done—in manufacturing as well as in all sectors.

Implications Going Forward

We have told the stories in this chapter to bring home a few key points. Embedded intelligence can be both powerful and baffling. Many, many factors may need to be dealt with when you're trying to implement the technology. And in that respect, embedded systems are really no different from other kinds of IT systems a company might wish to use.

Embedded intelligence can be both powerful and baffling.

Good solutions come from a blend of deep computing knowledge with keen business sense. For best results, you've got to have businesspeople and IT people working together effectively. And from this point, let's dive into how such synergy can be achieved. We'll start by diagnosing common problems that arise, then move into practical solutions.

CHAPTER 7:

Bridging the Gap Between IT and Business: Problems and Solutions

P ick a number. If you search the Web for "how many major information technology projects fail?" or something similar, you will find different statistics from various sources. Right now, we're looking at a survey that says about 66 percent of long-term IT and software development projects fail. Another source, an industry expert, hedges his bets by citing a wide range: he estimates "a failure range fluctuating between 25 and 85 percent." The sources mentioned earlier, in chapter 1, put the figure at the high end of this range.

None of the numbers are reassuring. They're bad enough to make a company not even want to try. We are intimately familiar with the problems since our firm is often called into situations where a project has stalled or gone off the rails. Drawing from firsthand experience, we offer this chapter and the next one as a guide to answering two questions: What typically goes wrong? And how can these failures be fixed or, better yet, avoided and replaced with success stories?

The Nature and Roots of "Failure"

Let's start by getting clear on exactly what a "failed" IT project means. It does not necessarily mean your company gets nothing for the money and time invested—although sometimes it does. In those cases, a project is killed, and you are back to a state far behind square one. You are at square less-than-zero, out millions of dollars and immersed in a sea of bad feelings and blame-placing, with nothing to show for it.

But a more common failure mode is that a major project *fails to meet its stated objectives*. The end product does not deliver the expected functionality, or it's full of bugs. The project runs significantly over budget or behind schedule. Sometimes all of these outcomes arrive together in a big, unhappy package, with effects that can be even worse than a dead project.

A classic case was the trouble-filled launch of the US government website HealthCare.gov in 2013. The site and the IT systems behind it were needed for implementing the Affordable Care Act, meant to provide access to health insurance for uninsured Americans. But when the long-announced enrollment period began on October 1 of that year, the site and systems were not ready. The website couldn't handle the volume of visitor traffic to begin with. People who managed to log in found basic functions like pull-down menus not working consistently. Private insurance companies that were part of the plan weren't linked into the system properly. Frustrations abounded, and although the problems were eventually fixed, comprehensive fixes took many months and IT costs ran well over the projected budget. As one news source put it when reporting on the follow-up investigation: "Failures by management and poor communication doomed the HealthCare.gov site from the start."[8]

One may be tempted to write off this fiasco as a product of inefficient government bureaucracy. But we at CG Infinity have seen the same sorts of issues arise repeatedly in private-sector businesses. Here's one example out of many:

A client of ours, a fine industrial services company, developed a handy mobile app for its field inspectors. Unfortunately, the app had a habit of crashing at crucial times. Angry field reps were demanding the CIO's head on a platter. The company called us instead, asking for help.

The best we could do was an emergency repair. Working with the company's IT team, we found and plugged the software leaks that were causing the crashes. However, we had to warn the company's executives that problems would soon resurface. The app's architecture was inherently flawed, sure to slip again. It needed a comprehensive rewrite.

And whose fault was that? Time after time, in cases like this, we find that the short answer is "probably everyone's." When IT projects fail to deliver expected results, the roots can often be traced to gaps in communication and coordination between the information technology people and the business leaders. They misunderstand each other. Projects begin on an unstable footing with unrealistic expectations or impractical game plans. This makes a hard job harder from the start, virtually assuring that problems will arise, and then when they do, the parties lose trust in each other as well.

Let's look at some common gaps and forms of failure. Along the way, we'll point out better approaches that could help to build the foundations for success.

---

8   This is from "Probe Finds Reasons for Obamacare Website Failure," *Inc.*, July 31, 2014, https://www.inc.com/associated-press/management-failure-results-in-healthcare.gov-woes.html, which was reprinted from an Associated Press story.

Language Gaps = Thinking Gaps

It has been noted that IT people and businesspeople speak different languages. The CIO or head of IT speaks in tech jargon, while the CEO and CFO speak the language of market share and return on investment, and the heads of marketing and sales beat the drum for enhancing "customer experience." To the extent that this disconnect occurs, it is more than a matter of the sides using different words.

If we were to get philosophical, we might quote the philosopher Martin Heidegger: "Language is the house of being." The language we use reflects our way of being in the world and how we think about the world. In IT projects, the IT side and the business side often seem to be living on different planets.

In IT projects, the IT side and the business side often seem to be living on different planets.

We know of one company that scheduled a top-level project review meeting. The CIO showed up believing he was superbly well prepared. He had a status report nearly thirty pages long, detailing where his IT team stood on each and every task related to development of the software. The question was not whether the CFO understood these details; the question was whether he cared about the report at all. The CFO was visibly tuned out and turned off. His concern was the money sunk into a project already missing milestones for deliverables. He wanted to know when and how he could expect the whole thing to pay off … and who could be found to replace the current CIO in order to get the result.

What could have been done better? Many things, but we'll point out two, one for each side of the gap.

- Of course, the CIO knew the project was falling behind. It appears that he took the steps that—to his mind, and in his view of the world—added up to the best possible solution: namely, getting a precise handle on the status of all the technical issues. Perhaps he expected his report to be an ironclad defense from that standpoint. It would demonstrate how firmly he was in command of the foundering ship. But given what the CFO (and probably others) cared about, perhaps a better approach would've been to think in terms of collaboration rather than defense.

  He could have thought, and said, something along these lines: "Hey, I know we're behind the curve on this project. My team is trying to get on top of the technical problems, and I can show you the details if you want. But I think the main thing we need to do is put our heads together and figure out the best way forward. Can you give me some guidance? If I explain where we're stuck, and if each of you explain your issues, can we work out a way to support each other and get to where the company needs to be?"

Now for the business side of the table:

- Some companies churn through CIOs the way a struggling football team churns through head coaches and quarterbacks. They bring in a new person, give that person just enough time to fail, and then look for someone else to be the savior. This is a telltale symptom of a lack of trust, a subject we'll say more about shortly. More fundamentally, though, it suggests that shuffling personnel is not the solution to chronic underperformance on IT projects. Business executives are best advised to look at their entire approaches to planning and monitoring these projects.

To begin with, the top people on the business side need a working grasp of what a digitization project consists of. This does not mean they must be able to write or understand code as well as hard-core techies do. They should, however, be able to see the IT tech staff (and/or a team of consultants) as more than a black box into which they can put requirements and expect solutions to come out the other end.

In fact, speaking of requirements, a good place to start building bridges is by understanding how a software-intensive project is different from other projects that a company might undertake.

Why Software Is Not Like Other Things

Every IT project begins with a set of "requirements." In many cases, they are written out formally. In organizations that adopt an agile development process, they may be implicit in "user stories" describing how someone would use the product. Either way, there are initial requirements that amount to firm expectations. The company wants a new platform or application that will do this, this, and this for the users. Marketing wants to bring out a new product with features x, y, and z. That sort of statement or intention is always present at the start.

But almost inevitably, once the project gets underway, it turns out that certain requirements need to change. Often, this greatly annoys the business heads, who are used to setting objectives and managing to those objectives, not seeing them shift beneath their feet. Changing requirements also lead to delays and undermine the credibility of the IT people, who are seen as incapable of following through on a simple plan. It must be understood why software requirements can change for any or all of several reasons.

To begin with, software is literally a code: a model of reality, which works by translating human concepts into the binary language of zeros and ones. (Those are the only "words" that the tiny transistors in chips can understand. To put it simply, each one switches the current on or off at particular times, depending on whether it sees a 0 or a 1 signal.) The fact that there can be *billions* of transistors in a single CPU chip—and that by doing their on-and-off dances together with other circuit elements, they can give you directions to the nearest Indian restaurant or play chess—is truly mind-boggling. Most mortals should not try to ponder how such things are possible.

What's important is to recognize that in this seemingly magical realm, some things may not be possible. Requirements are stated in "high-level" human language, which includes general concepts we all understand: We want to "calculate" the "average" of some numbers or find the "shortest route" through "traffic," or display "colors" in hues from "violet" to "red." Sometimes, our groupings of such terms cannot be translated down to workable sets of zeros and ones. Or it turns out they can't be rendered that way without throwing off other parts of the code. So this is one factor that can cause a need to change requirements.

Consider, too, that any new software is meant for uses new to the company. If it's to be offered to customers in a new market for entry into the market, there may well be unknowns in that market that only come to light gradually. Meanwhile, the state of the art in software and microelectronics keeps changing. Both are relatively young sciences, making it still harder to have requirements and objectives set in stone. A cool feature that would give you a competitive edge today might be obsolete tomorrow, or it might be standard stuff that everybody has, which means you need to aim higher.

In short, a major digitization project has lots of moving parts as well as moving targets. The work is demanding in multiple dimensions, and moreover, the complexity of it is not easily perceptible. Unlike a big construction project in the physical world where you can *see* what a massive endeavor it is, all you see when you walk into an IT department is a bunch of people hunched over screens. The software itself is invisible.

These strange qualities tend to aggravate divisions that already exist in a company. Nonspecialists grow suspicious of IT while failing to appreciate its unique demands. The IT people feel pressured and may also feel as if they're confined to an enclave, with little power to influence the overall strategic direction of the company. And yet both sides need each other. As we have shown repeatedly in the previous case-study chapters of this book, every business today is an IT business. A company's only choices are to get the IT aspect and the business aspects working together, or to fall progressively further behind.

Let's pull back for an initial overview of some measures that can help to bring harmony to the scene and make major IT projects more likely to succeed.

What Works and What Doesn't: Some Pivotal Factors

By drawing on what is widely known about IT projects, we can highlight some factors that lead a project to succeed or not. By combining this knowledge with themes you've seen us identify in stories about our clients, we can recommend some steps for moving the needle in a positive direction. All is summarized in table 7-1.

TABLE 7-1: FOUR KEYS TO IT PROJECTS

WHAT MATTERS	SUCCESS FACTORS	FAILURE FACTORS	HOW TO DO BETTER
Size	Smaller projects have higher success rates.	Success rates decrease as projects grow larger and more complex.	Divide big projects into manageable chunks, starting small and simple.
Duration	Shorter-term projects are more likely to hit the original targets.	Long-term projects are more prone to diverge from plan as things change and new issues arise.	Slot the chunks of work into short time periods, with any course corrections to be made at the end of each.
Communication	Best results come from mixing informal communication channels with the formal project management process.	Overfocus on formal communication can lead to missing the clues about a problem before it becomes one.	Understand and address the undercurrents. Detect the tremors before the earthquake.
Empathy	Mutual understanding, trust, and respect between IT and other parts of the firm.	Absence or breakdown of trust and respect.	Communicate early and often, always with an eye to problem-solving together.

The first three recommendations in the right-hand "How to Do Better" column should be familiar to you from preceding chapters. Divide and conquer is a proven strategy for cutting big jobs down to size, and it applies both to parceling out the work and to scheduling it stepwise in time. The CEO of the energy trading firm in chapter 4 scheduled the Web-based digitization of his company into quarterly time periods. This established a good working cadence while providing regular checkpoints to assess progress toward the ultimate goal.

We've also seen IT leaders apply the concept somewhat differently. One person stepped into a tough situation as the new CIO at a company where prior projects hadn't gone well. He knew he needed to build trust right away. So the first project he tackled was small enough that he could show results in two to three weeks. The next set of projects he picked up were doable in four to six weeks, again with measurable results. Confidence level in the new CIO began to climb. He didn't push his luck, but he kept moving up the scale, taking on and completing progressively larger pieces of work. Eventually, he was able to propose, and get millions of dollars in funding for, a two-year project that would upgrade a substantial part of the company's operations.

But there was more to this person's success story than simply starting out small and going bigger. Consider the last recommendation under "How to Do Better" in table 7-1: "Communicate early and often, always with an eye to problem-solving together." Probably none of the CIO's projects would have succeeded unless he'd also been able to communicate and collaborate positively with the people heading up other parts of the firm.

That ongoing interaction is absolutely essential. And, as we emphasized in earlier chapters, it has to run deeper than periodic formal meetings or exchanges in which requirements and progress reports are handed over the wall between departments. The relevant leaders in the company—from IT and from marketing, finance, product engineering, or wherever—need to build true working relationships. The kind in which one party can get input or assistance from the other on short notice. The kind in which business leaders gain at least an elementary understanding of what can and cannot be done with information technology and vice versa. The kind of relationship that enables each party to begin *thinking* in the other's terms, so that they can create synergies instead of bumping into one another like half-blind mice in a maze.

Bridging the Gap All the Way—or Why Partial Bridges Will Not Suffice

Building such relationships is difficult for many of us. Most IT leaders are not trained for the task. As graduates of computer-intensive university programs or technical schools, they are conditioned to keep their eyes on the screen and their heads in the bits and bytes. Courses in user experience design or human-computer interaction are about as far their education goes into the personal sphere, and their work experience usually doesn't help much in this regard, either. Often the most competent technical person is promoted to CIO. Little thought is given to whether that person is prepared to think and interact in business terms.

Thus, it often falls upon the business leaders, particularly the CEO, to initiate and orchestrate the bridge-building. We would urge you to pursue it to the fullest. We have seen companies take partial measures and wind up with an organization that's out of alignment.

Here is one example. The company wanted to launch an ambitious digitization project that involved creating new customer-facing Web services and thereby opening up potential new revenue streams. The CIO was not eager to lead the project. His view of IT was a traditional one. He saw the role of IT as providing internal G&A services: managing the intranet and the databases, looking after security, and so forth.

The top business executives decided to form a separate unit dedicated to the big project. They recruited a permanent leader for it and funded a team. The move worked out just as they had hoped, except for one problem. Before long, the company had an excellent suite of Web services up and running, which customers loved and were willing to pay for. But that is where the problem arose. Functions like order processing and the keeping of customer accounts didn't live in the new project unit. They lived over the wall, in the G&A-type systems managed by the CIO. The company had dual IT systems that were not seamlessly integrated, along with what amounted to dual IT departments, each consuming a sizable portion of payroll and managerial attention. Merging the two would prove to be yet another major project.

This story is especially relevant, as more than a few companies have begun taking similar steps by appointing a separate C-level person—usually titled the CDO: chief digital officer—to head ambitious digitization work. That may be fine as far as it goes. The question is whether it goes far enough in the right direction. Unless the CDO and the CDO's domain are working in concert with those of the CIO and the business executives, there is a risk of proliferating disconnects and frictions instead of solving them.

The moral of the story is that halfway bridges won't give you the optimum. It's best to go all the way, aiming for seamless integration of both digital systems and human systems through the building of deep relationships between your IT leader and business leaders. Let's look deeply into this essential subject.

CHAPTER 8:

Bridging the Gap: Building Relationships That Work

One fact of business life should be very clear by now. To stay competitive in years ahead, your company will *repeatedly* need to undertake digitization projects that go beyond business as usual. Some will be aimed at putting you ahead of the competition through creative uses of technology, while others will be necessary upgrades. And on each of those projects, the working relationships between your digitization leader and other C-level executives will be either a key success factor or a key failure factor.

> *To stay competitive ... your company will repeatedly need to undertake digitization projects that go beyond business as usual.*

This chapter digs into the fundamentals of building working relationships that work. The goal is to do more than resolve conflicts or slippages between the two "sides" of the company. It's to create a company that is fluent at using information technology proactively: a company where state-of-the-art IT can be integrated with business strategy to gain the maximum possible leverage in the market and produce maximum impact on the bottom line. In short, this is about building a foundation that will let you aim high.

The foundation is built by bringing the leadership team, including the IT leader, into a state of dynamic alignment. All must be able to work together smoothly in the present while co-anticipating and co-capitalizing upon new developments. If that sounds far from what currently exists in your company, don't be discouraged. There are steps you can take on the human level, as well as on the level of policies and procedures, to move toward a dynamic fusion of information technology and business.

The first step is understanding who must be in charge of this fusion.

The CEO's Role: Like a Movie Producer, Like the Hub of a Wheel

On any project that is more than a routine upgrading of IT infrastructure—on a project designed to exploit a business opportunity, to create a competitive advantage, to launch a new business model, or to reinvent the company—there has to be someone in the middle, pulling everything together. And that someone has to be the CEO, because only the CEO has the authority to make everyone coordinate with each other. Only the CEO has the credibility and the position to overcome resistance to change, whether that inertia exists at the top of the company on the board, or whether it's down in the organization.

Ideally, the project will flow like a symphony played by a great orchestra. The music swells and diminishes at times, but the composition moves ever forward as the various players come in just when they should, weaving grand harmonies. In this context, it's tempting to think of the CEO's role in digitization as being like an orchestra conductor: the maestro who stands front and center above everyone, directing traffic. But a much better analogy comes from another art form.

The role is similar to that of a movie producer. You may not even know who the producers were on your favorite films since they operate behind the scenes and don't often make headlines. (The exceptions are the multifaceted producer-writer-director types like the Coen brothers, who do so much of the hands-on work themselves that they're just called "filmmakers.") But in every case, the producer is the person who stands in the middle of a complex production and sees that it all comes together.

The producer coordinates the efforts of high-powered people who are creative leaders in their own specialties: the star actors; the screenwriter, director, and cinematographer; the special effects wizards and the heads of the technical teams. All may have their own often conflicting ideas about what should be done. And all tend to think that their needs and views should take priority. *In addition* to orchestrating that circus, the producer must also deal with the money people and with those who will market and distribute the film, who likewise have their own views and priorities.

Is it any wonder that so many movies turn out looking like tangled messes? Some result from good ideas that got pulled out of shape by competing agendas. Or bold ideas that got bogged down into boring mediocrity. On the bright side, some succeed smashingly if the producer has coordinated well.

That's the role the CEO must play in digitization projects. And it really is no different from what a good CEO does in other aspects of the company's business—being the point person on strategic direction and also the ringleader who ensures that everybody aligns around implementing the strategy. Often the CEO delegates a lot of the latter part to a COO. But the main message still holds true.

Whenever a company sets out on any substantially new course—*which includes major digitization*—it's up to the CEO to do three things:

- Take a comprehensive, 360-degree view of the venture.

- See that all key players are in the loop, contributing and collaborating in an all-around team effort.

- Maintain the momentum. Don't let anything stall or sidetrack the company's movement to a new way of doing business.

Moreover, since the future is likely to require more than one significant digitization project, the issue needs to be tackled on more than a one-off basis. What a smart company will do is establish a foundational framework and conditions for ongoing, progressively more advanced digitization. That is a lot of jargon in one sentence, so let's visualize it.

FIGURE 8-1: DT COLLABORATION FRAMEWORK

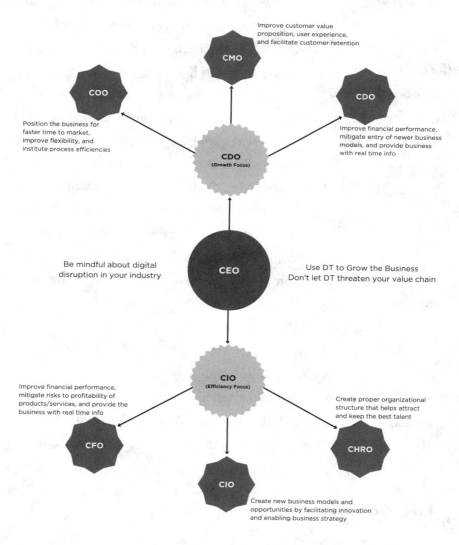

Digital Transformation (DT) Collaboration Framework

In organization-chart terms, figure 8-1 shows what the overall arrangement would look like for digitization in a typical company. Notice that it's not a hierarchical, top-down framework. Instead, you could say it represents the "wheel of progress" that has to be created and set in motion for projects to succeed. The CEO is at the hub, asking the big strategic questions about how to use digital *technology* for maximum *business* advantage. But the CEO is not alone in this regard. Digital/business thinking radiates out to all the key leaders in the organization. They're all looking at what they could do to leverage digital technology in their parts of the business.

> *The CEO is at the hub, asking the big strategic questions about how to use digital technology for maximum business advantage.*

Out of that interactive group practice will come coherent, well-rounded strategies and projects for moving forward, which then will, in fact, move forward—again, with the CEO at the hub, getting everyone to work together to make the wheel roll straight and true.

Now, of course, real life is never as simple as it's shown in diagrams and flowcharts. Therefore, while keeping figure 8-1 in mind, we now leave the realm of idealized visualization. We're going to walk through the real-life steps that a CEO (and the CEO's leadership team) can take to build the framework and conditions for ongoing digitization.

The Basics

A good working relationship is like a good marriage or friendship in several respects. For example, it depends on open, productive communication. However, that is not the starting point. Learning a bundle of communication techniques won't get you anywhere unless the underlying groundwork is done. So let's begin from the beginning.

- In any relationship, choosing the right partner is step one. For a business, this means having an appropriate person in place as the CIO or otherwise-titled head of digitization.

- Good relationships are also marked by *mutual understanding* of one another and a *shared vision of where the relationship is meant to go.* Just as a marriage works best when the spouses agree on the kind of life they'd like to have, a company in the Digital Age works best when the digital leader understands and supports the business goals, while conversely, the business leaders understand what can and cannot be done with digital technologies. These are the areas where active relationship-building is typically needed.

- Along with the above come the details of communication. The IT and business heads literally need to practice productive ways of talking with each other. And concurrent with that ...

- The CEO (with help from the C-suite) can set guidelines that promote ongoing collaboration within a simple, nonbureaucratic framework that channels everybody's efforts toward bottom-line impact on EBITDA.

These steps will require effort, but not onerous effort, and if they are done well, the results should provide generous payback on the work put in. You are making the company more fundamentally fit for a world in which "every business is an IT business." Let's look at each action area in some depth.

Choosing an Appropriate CIO

Here are some observations that apply equally well to evaluating a current IT leader or seeking a new one. The person who fills this role must have three capabilities, or at least the potential to develop them quickly on the job:

a. Understanding the company's business in a deeper than superficial sense.

b. A firm command of how to *plan and direct* an IT project in pursuit of the company's business goals.

c. The personal qualities needed for collaborating with people from other disciplines.

Almost anyone can get an elementary understanding of a company's business just by reading articles on the Web. "The company is in such-and-such industry. It's a price-driven industry (or a high-growth industry, or whatever), which means you need to control costs (or focus on growth, etc.) ..." This level of business knowledge is not enough. The IT leader has to be capable of grasping the finer points behind the big picture, such as these: Exactly how do the CEO and CFO intend to grow the company or cut costs? How does that fit with the market trends and the competitive landscape? What plans do the chief marketing and sales officers have for acquiring and retaining customers? How can the company market itself in ways that will be heard through the noise and clutter?

It's important that the IT leader be able to tune into these matters because information technology *can help with all of them*. And, in order to help, the IT leader must also have the skills required for taking the relevant business knowledge into the IT team and planning and directing projects that will provide the needed functionality.

Sadly, more than a few companies have wound up with CIOs who are not up to either of these mission-critical tasks. In many cases, the post was filled by promoting the most technically competent person on the IT staff. Technical experts are extremely valuable in the role of solving wicked technical problems, and they deserve to be rewarded for their skills, but raising such persons to a high-level executive position often does nobody a favor. The experts are Peter Principled out of their areas of expertise. While they may be familiar with standard business functions like routine accounting, which corporate IT systems are designed to support, they tend to have little exposure to the more sophisticated aspects of doing business competitively.

Nor are they likely to be expert at directing the IT staff. It's well known in the software world that the best developers do not necessarily make good project managers for the same reason that great athletes don't necessarily become great head coaches. The required skill sets are different. And if a technical guru-turned-CIO also happens to struggle with the interpersonal skills of collaborating across departments, everyone loses on all fronts. The company is left with the classic gap between the IT and business sides, which can have toxic effects on big projects.

But take heart. There are some ways to get a good person on the job, including the way that we most often recommend.

WHAT MIGHT WORK ... AND WHAT IS MORE LIKELY TO WORK

Let's begin with two common approaches and look at the caveats that go with them. We mentioned one approach at the end of the previous chapter, which is to have dual IT leaders: a chief information officer for handling the routine stuff and a chief digital officer (or some such title) to lead the bigger, bolder digitization projects. This can work but it is not a panacea. To begin with, CDOs are human too. They tend to have their own shortcomings. Further, as noted before, dividing the company's IT operations may create separate fiefdoms, each in charge of systems and functions that aren't well integrated with one another. And above all, we'd leave you with this caveat. *Naming a CDO should never be seen as a substitute for the CEO's responsibility to coordinate major digitization.* While the CDO is expected to bring certain skills to the party, the company's top executive must always be at the center, seeing that the IT leader(s) and business leaders work in harmony to make big projects work.

A second approach to achieving this harmony is choosing an IT-savvy businessperson as the CIO. This also can work, but it may instead just push the gap between business and IT down into the IT department, between the CIO and the CIO's staff. Naturally, many businesspeople today have a better-than-average working knowledge of information technology. They have been using computers and software in their own work. They may know how to write code. Yet it's still hard for such persons to be aware of all the considerations that go into a complex, enterprise-level digitization project.

Implementing a business solution in bits and bytes is not easy, especially not within an IT system that's already full of intricate inter-dependencies and things that will break if they're tweaked the wrong way. Lacking deep knowledge of this environment, the business-oriented CIO is prone to make unreasonable decisions, like "We're going to launch a new B2C channel in three months," which the IT staff knows will not be doable. Trust is lost, targets aren't met, and the company is again left with the toxic gap issue.

The ideal IT leader really does need to be a Renaissance person—someone who can understand disparate worlds well enough to connect them and make them sing. And since ideal candidates rarely come ready made, a company is best advised to go with a bright, adaptive person who is strong in one area and trainable in the rest. *In our experience, this should usually be someone with the technical expertise in place.* That kind of CIO can quickly earn the respect of the IT team and is less likely to lead a project down a blind alley. Equally important, a tech-based IT leader will be much better equipped to represent the full range of possibilities that digital technology can offer when interacting with the company's business leaders.

Therefore, a sensible order for many companies is first to settle on a CIO who is technically strong and shows promise of growing into the rest of the position. The next steps are then bringing that person up to speed business-wise, and setting the stage for true collaboration between business and IT.

Toward Mutual Understanding: Steps for Acclimating the CIO

A CIO cannot learn all the important points of a company's business during a training or orientation session of a few days. So, while a formal business-education program of some sort can be a good introduction, the CIO needs to learn ongoingly, organically, and (one would hope) rapidly.

Education specialists often make a distinction between two kinds of learning: "just in case" and "just in time." Just-in-case learning is the type that typically occurs in a college classroom. You learn a great deal about a subject area up front, just in case you may need some of it later on. Just-in-time learning is what typically happens on the job. A situation comes up or is on the horizon that you will need to comprehend and handle. An experienced colleague gives you the context and explains how it's done. Then you move on to another just-in-time occasion, and another. This form of learning is believed by many to be more efficient as well as more hands-on, which helps it to stick. One drawback is that you don't want to be learning just in time in emergency mode, when the pressure and the stakes are high. You may not have adequate time to digest what you are learning. You are liable to get only part of the picture and make costly mistakes.

There is a simple variation on the just-in-time approach that avoids this pitfall while incorporating further advantages. For a CIO learning the company's business side, it would work as follows:

REQUIRE THE CIO TO MEET INFORMALLY, BUT REGULARLY, WITH EACH OF THE KEY BUSINESS LEADERS IN THE COMPANY.

They can meet for coffee, over lunch, or at any time that's mutually convenient. The CIO can ask about specific topics that seem puzzling. The business executive can ask about equivalent topics in information technology. Both can talk open-endedly about what's new or important in their fields. The learning becomes a two-way exchange. It happens sort of just in time but not under pressure and has the added benefit of helping to build personal bonds between the CIO and the others on the C-level team. We highly recommend this process.

And we have a suggestion for bridging differences at times when the pressure is high. These can arise frequently during the course of a project. For instance, the CIO or IT representative is trying to think and problem-solve in one direction while the businessperson comes at it from another angle entirely. In such cases, it's wise to have a preappointed mediator close at hand. We call this mediator an "honest broker."

The honest broker can be someone whose expertise (and allegiance) leans primarily to one side but can be trusted to lead both sides toward resolution. You have at least one person in your company who would qualify. Put that individual to work, brokering honestly across the gap.

Toward Mutual Understanding: What the "Business Side" Can Do

In many companies, there tends to be a focus on addressing the deficiencies of the CIO. The prevailing attitude goes something like this: "What can we do to drill some business sense into this guy?" That's a faulty attitude. It speaks to only half of the gap while ignoring the other half.

On your side—the business side—you have a couple of key obligations, and it's up to the CEO to see that these are met.

One is to acquire a basic understanding of what is possible and not possible with information technology. If every business today is truly an IT business—and there is plenty of evidence behind the statement—then how can you and your team run a business without a working knowledge of IT? You can't. The state of the art keeps advancing too. Among other things, you should be aware of your company's "technology deficit": the places where you are behind the curve or your systems lack what's needed to keep running properly. One example could be an out-of-date ERP system, for which you've been deferring an update because it is a huge task.

KNOWING THE FUNDAMENTALS OF INFORMATION TECHNOLOGY AND STAYING ON TOP OF NEW DEVELOPMENTS HAS TO BE PART OF THE JOB DESCRIPTION FOR EVERY KEY EXECUTIVE IN A MODERN COMPANY.

Another obligation is for the people on the business side to be on the same page. If you want the CIO and the IT department to support your business goals, you cannot give them mixed messages as to what those goals are. We have seen this kind of mixed messaging repeatedly.

One company we've worked with is a well-respected maker of consumer goods for the home. For years, the company sold its products through a variety of retail stores, some of them company-owned, along with chain retailers and independent local outlets. But then, as ecommerce ate into bricks-and-mortar retail, those channels began to weaken. Long-trusted sales partners were either cutting back their orders or closing.

To survive, the company planned multiple moves. One was to greatly upgrade its Web presence for direct sales to consumers, and another was to reduce costs without losing quality. The latter included consolidation of manufacturing, which had been done in the United States at a number of regional plants that would be combined into a few larger ones.

Now imagine being the company's CIO. The marketing and sales executives want the customer-facing Web work done ASAP to get revenue flowing. The people in manufacturing urgently need their parts of the IT systems to be reworked so they can provide high-quality products to sell. Meanwhile, the head of logistics is altering supply chains and warehousing to go with the new manufacturing setup, and those systems need reworking too. It is a type of situation any company might face in today's fast-changing markets. But here is the CIO, bombarded by competing, urgent demands. And to complicate things further, all demands involve IT functions that will have to be integrated with each other—and with the systems of third-party providers—in order to achieve a reliable cadence of customers placing online orders that are then filled and delivered promptly.

In cases like this, bringing order to the confusion (or better yet, preventing it in the first place) is the job of the CEO. Only the company's top person has the authority to pull together the executives and have them work out a unified, prioritized agenda to present to the CIO. It is the CIO's job to push back on this agenda from a technical viewpoint, if needed, and to come up with a workable plan for meeting the various objectives step by step. Overall, someone also needs to keep a big-picture eye on the issue of systems integration, and the CIO should take the lead in that regard as well.

> *Bringing order to the confusion (or better yet, preventing it in the first place) is the job of the CEO.*

But even so, we'd like to bring the emphasis back to the responsibilities on the business side. Both the project planning and the big-picture integration will go better when the business leaders are active, supportive participants from day one. Initiatives that affect the entire company need to be shaped by representatives of the entire company, even when they are technical initiatives led by the head of IT. There's simply no escaping the imperative to work together in the ways that we have been describing.

Communication Skills

A couple of basic communication tips may be helpful too. One big thing that helps in communicating with IT people is telling them not just what you want to have done, but also why. Very often, we hear business leaders voicing a need without sharing the reasons behind it. "We need a new website." The IT leader may get the message, but you're most likely to be happy with the results if you spell out what the site is expected to accomplish for the company. Then the IT team can target their efforts more efficiently. They can ask relevant questions, and they may indeed come up with ideas you hadn't thought of. A key point to keep in mind is the following:

> *The IT leader and key IT people are doers and compet-itors. They want to win, just as an aggressive business leader does. Given the chance, they're eager to show that they can build best-of-breed websites and systems. Fully sharing the "whys" behind a project will help give them that chance to excel.*

The other communication tip is simply to listen. In particular, listen to objections that the IT leader raises in relation to business plans. Of course, it is possible the person is trying to bargain you down to an easier task, thereby dodging what looks like a stretch goal for the IT staff. But the objections are much more likely to be real. When a technically competent CIO says, "It can't be done," or "This will cause serious problems," are you willing to bet that it's safe to forge ahead anyway? We would usually put our money on the CIO.

You don't have to agree with everything the person says. By all means, challenge objections that you think are unfounded. But the dialogue is essential. And to have a dialogue, one must listen.

The Next Steps from Here

For eight chapters, we've shared insights and advice. Implementation is up to you. The next chapter, our final one, offers a suggested template for moving forward.

CHAPTER 9:

A Roadmap to the Future

Tradition says to close a book with a recap of the main messages. But the real need is to move forward quickly and decisively. So the main messages here are woven into a recommended plan for leveraging IT to move a company ahead.

This chapter is aimed primarily at the CEO. It's also useful to anyone with strategic responsibility. While the IT strategy that you adopt will, of course, be specific to your company, we can point to some underlying principles that apply everywhere. First and foremost:

WHEN THINKING ABOUT HOW YOUR COMPANY COULD USE INFORMATION TECHNOLOGY, KEEP IN MIND THAT EVERYTHING IS AT STAKE AND ALMOST ANYTHING IS POSSIBLE.

Many, many companies have been wiped out by failing to prepare for new uses of IT. Conversely, many have thrived by leveraging and combining these uses in ways that were once beyond imagining. Just looking at the phone you carry—a nearly miraculous device, for which the name "phone" doesn't begin to capture everything it does—should serve as a reminder to stretch your thinking.

The possibilities of what any company could do are, if not infinite, far vaster than the average business plan. And it behooves you to be on the right side of those possibilities. Between thriving and being wiped out, there may not be much middle ground. Therefore:

- Having a well-thought-out IT strategy is essential. This strategy should enable, and be intertwined with, the company's strategic *business* goals.

- The business goals shouldn't be just the usual or predictable ones. The company's leaders need to think expansively of how new uses of digital technology could create opportunities (or threats) that otherwise might not exist.

- Finally, every digital initiative should in some way contribute to growing the bottom line. Certainly, the company should reap some near-term gains. But at the same time, it is necessary to target potential long-term gains—the kind that could come from building sustainable competitive advantage in blue-sky, Blue Ocean markets.

Every digital initiative should in some way contribute to growing the bottom line.

Now for a suggested action plan. Based on our long experience with midsized companies as described in the previous chapters of this book, we believe you will find it well worth your time to undertake a four-step process that goes generally as follows:

1. Evaluate where your company stands now in terms of leveraging IT.

2. Develop a vision of where you'd like to be.

3. Align the C-suite team around that vision.

4. Then strategize and implement.

If you would like to undertake this process interactively with us, we can direct you to a CG Infinity website for the purpose. It's free of charge. The site will walk you through the initial stages and offer guidance for the rest, along with reference and support material. Meanwhile, here is a closer look at each of the four suggested steps.

Step 1: Evaluate Where You Stand

Often a good process begins with benchmarking. When it comes to leveraging IT for bottom-line impact, you can benchmark your company against the current competition in your market … or against what is possible to do with the technology.

We recommend benchmarking in terms of what's possible. Markets and industries are likely to change in the months and years ahead. New competitors may come in from seemingly nowhere. And, as was shown in chapter 2, conventional survival strategies won't cut it in this environment. "Survival mode" typically means cutting costs across the board—including the cost of investment for the future—while hunkering down to protect one's present market position. Today, that is practically a formula for being overrun and left in the dust.

Survival requires aiming ahead of the curve: aiming for leadership. A company must "thrive to survive," playing to win instead of not to lose. And ominously, many midsized companies are not yet leveraging IT in ways that would empower them to do that.

See table 9-1, which is a reprint of the chart from chapter 2. It depicts the levels of maturity at which a company can operate in its uses of digital technology.

TABLE 9-1 (A COPY OF TABLE 2-1): WHERE DO YOU STAND IN TERMS OF LEVERAGING IT?

		CRAWL	WALK	RUN	FLY
Admin and Support Uses	Basic IT for internet, email, etc.	Yes	Yes	Yes	Yes
Sales and Marketing	Leverage IT to grow or maintain top line.		Yes	Yes	Yes
Cost of Goods Sold	Reduce cost of goods sold, improve gross profit margin			Yes	Yes
Expansion, Exponential Growth	Use IT to enter new markets, Blue Oceans.				Yes

Chances of marketplace survival increase *by moving this way.* >>

EBITDA is likely to grow *by moving this way.* >>

The companies most at risk are at the least mature level. They're moving at a crawl, as it were. *If your company views IT merely as a cost center*—as nothing more than a necessary part of the G&A overhead for keeping the books and for keeping people connected—the harsh reality is that you're just crawling. The good news is that you have plenty of upside ahead. There are many opportunities to pick up the pace and improve your outlook by moving to more advanced forms of IT leverage.

The next level for many companies is to leverage IT in sales and marketing. They're building a healthy online presence, perhaps using channels like social media, *and* they are using in-house IT tools to target, plan, and support their interactions with customers and prospects. If you are at this level, you're at least walking the walk of the Digital Age. But even here, as table 9-1 shows, there is still a huge upside waiting to be exploited. You can break into a run. Or better yet, take wing and fly.

Once more, we invite you to visit the CG Infinity website for an interactive walk-through of this evaluation exercise.

And then, after you have made a fair assessment of your company's current standing, you should be able to see at least the outlines of two important pictures. One is your vulnerability to being outpaced by companies that use IT more aggressively. The other is the opportunity that you have to be one of those leaders.

Now it is time to focus on the opportunity and flesh out the picture. The next step in the suggested four-step process is all about that.

Step 2: Develop a Vision

While it's true that every business today is an IT business, this does not mean that you have to be the most IT-intensive company in your industry in order to win. Digitization for its own sake rhymes with "mistake." The idea is to digitize selectively with criteria like these in mind:

> *Digitization for its own sake rhymes with "mistake." The idea is to digitize selectively.*

- **WHAT KIND OF DIGITAL INITIATIVE(S) COULD ENABLE YOU TO SERVE YOUR CUSTOMERS BETTER?** *And/or attract new customers?* What do they care about? What are their pain points? How could IT solve those pain points?

  Here, you're looking for ways to gain competitive advantage and grow top-line revenue by leveraging IT. Recall that in chapter 4, we saw an energy trading company grow dramatically by thinking customer first. The company focused on energy brokers as the key customers and then built a Web platform that addressed the brokers' pain points, such as by providing much faster turnaround times on quotes.

- **WHERE ARE YOU BEHIND THE CURVE IN USES OF INFORMATION TECHNOLOGY?** This is your company's technology deficit. If competitors have an IT infrastructure that allows them to operate more efficiently than you—or if they're offering products and services with more attractive IT-enabled features—then you will need to catch up soon, if not surpass them.

- **ARE THERE WAYS TO AMP UP MARKETING AND SALES WITH NEW OR SMARTER USES OF IT?** Again, the target is top-line revenue growth, and the book has cited several examples of how this can be done. In one case, a company faced the need to grow its ecommerce presence generally to replace revenue lost from the decline of bricks-and-mortar retail. Elsewhere we saw that even midsized firms can now afford AI tools that let them target their online marketing more effectively.

- **WHERE AND HOW COULD DIGITAL INITIATIVES CUT COSTS?** The question is more open-ended than it might look. Every company has many costs and many possible ways of reducing them. Often, it's possible to digitize in ways that reduce costs while also growing revenue. These are excellent opportunities to look for.

- **WHAT WOULD A BLUE-SKY FUTURE LOOK LIKE FOR YOUR COMPANY? AND HOW COULD IT HELP YOU GET THERE?** Maybe there are new markets you'd love to enter. Maybe you've spotted an emerging growth market that your company could serve, either with existing products or with new ones you might develop.

  Or perhaps your ultimate goal is simply to grow, whether it's by scaling up what you already do, by offering something more, and/or by acquisition. In chapter 3 we saw a regional bank growing out of necessity. The imperative for the bank was to grow or die due to the spread of big interstate banks and e-banks.

On reflection, you will probably find that digital technology is central to achieving any of your business goals. Putting sincere effort into this step of the four-step process will yield valuable results. The vision that you develop should give you a clearer (and, we hope, more ambitious) picture of what your business goals really are. It's a vision of the company you could become versus the company that you are now. And this vision will give you a starting-point view of the kinds of IT applications you'll want to deploy.

Some tricky factors need to be considered. For example, digital technologies themselves will continue to evolve and advance. You might see an opportunity to jump ahead by leveraging an emerging technology—perhaps one that has just come to market or is fast approaching that stage. At the same time, you'll want to avoid locking the company into technologies or platforms that may soon become obsolete. (If you are already dependent on such a system, it's a flashing danger sign of technology deficit.)

Developing this vision isn't likely to be something a CEO alone can do. It will require input from key people in the company. The vision will need reality-checking from the company's IT leader(s). Although many details may be worked out later—such as exactly which technologies to leverage for which purposes, and the expected costs and benefits of each—the overall guiding vision can't be a fantasy. Ideally it will live at the leading edge of the realm of the doable.

And developing the vision in concert with others should lead naturally to the next step in the process.

Step 3: Align the C-suite Team Around the Vision

Many of the company's leaders will have had input on certain aspects of the vision. Now they all need to get behind the whole thing. This is crucial. As shown in several places throughout the book, IT systems are full of interlocking interdependencies, just as the various business functions are. Moreover, the leaders of those functions may have conflicting or competing demands, and the IT leader needs to be able to work effectively with all of them.

Chapters 7 and 8 have addressed these predicaments and the best approaches to getting everyone to pull together. We won't try to repeat the chapters here. We would simply ask you to consult your short-term memory or flip back to those chapters, if needed. And then move on to the final step when ready.

Step 4: Strategize and Implement

Once everyone buys into the vision or to a mutually negotiated new version of it, the company should proceed *immediately* with turning the vision into reality. Don't wait. Time is a nonrenewable resource. Better to have it on your side instead of working against you. So begin right away, with the parts of the vision that are most accessible. Work out specific strategies for implementing them and then implement.

Some general guidelines that may help, all gleaned from earlier chapters, are these:

- Divide and conquer. Trying to implement the entire vision in one grand digital initiative is very unlikely to go well. You can start with the low-hanging fruit, the easiest parts to do … or with the parts that are needed most urgently, or that meet some other criteria of your choice. *Smaller, shorter-term projects* succeed more often than larger, long-term projects. (See table 7-1.)

- In addition to dividing up portions of the work, divide each project timewise into working-period chunks with meaningful milestones. A good working period is of relatively short duration. A good milestone, if met, produces tangible benefits in itself and, if not met, can point the way to course corrections that might be needed.

Proceeding in this manner has several advantages. It maintains morale and provides near-term paybacks on money and time invested. It allows you to iterate and adjust both your IT strategies and your goals as you go along. It avoids the risk of going far, far down the road of developing systems that won't work right or may even turn out not to be needed.

- Finally, a point of advice for the CEO. *Let your leaders lead* in the areas that they know best. Your optimum role is to be like the movie producer in chapter 7, coordinating the enterprise without micromanaging it. And the task that only the CEO can do is to lay the groundwork for true collaboration between the company's business leaders and IT leaders, as described in chapter 8.

Will there still be points of contention? Of course. Mistakes will still be made, too, in the process of trying to leverage information technology to meet business goals. Working with fast-changing technologies in a fast-moving business environment practically guarantees that you will fall short of perfection. But we aren't promising perfection.

We do suggest that by applying the insights from this book, you can avoid bet-the-company mistakes and instead make smart strategic bets on the uses of information technology for bottom-line impact.

Remember the action-movie superheroes way back at the start of chapter 1? They became heroic by learning to use their superpowers wisely, for the good of all. Information technology is a superpower. May you use it to achieve your highest and best purposes!

About the Authors

BHOPI DHALL, FOUNDER AND CEO OF CG INFINITY

Bhopi's career has paralleled the evolution of modern IT. As an engineer and engineering manager at Texas Instruments from 1969 to 1997, he did cutting-edge work on the building blocks of advanced computing. As the head of CG Infinity, he has led projects involving business applications of AI, data mining, mobile technology, and more. Many clients have found the scope of his expertise to be a rare asset, producing digital solutions that are both innovative and fundamentally sound.

Bhopi earned a bachelor's degree in electrical engineering from the Indian Institute of Technology Bombay and a master's in electrical engineering from Michigan Tech. He joined Texas Instruments at a time when the company was building expansively on its early, pioneering work in integrated circuits. At TI, Bhopi and his team wrote key software for one of the world's first supercomputers. Bhopi also played lead roles in developing systems for air traffic control, digital light processing, GPS, and image recognition. He left to found CG Infinity (originally called Cyber Group) in 1998. At first, the firm consulted on engineering projects in areas such as intelligent automation and then gradually moved to its present focus on IT for business. Bhopi has grown CG Infinity to the point where it now employs over three hundred skilled specialists at locations across the United States and in India.

SAURAJIT KANUNGO, PRESIDENT OF CG INFINITY

Saurajit combines thirty-plus years of experience in business systems and project management with his expertise in IT. He emphasizes proactive strategic planning in the use of technology and has personally led large-scale, multiyear digital transformation initiatives, as well as many short-turnaround projects targeted to specific business goals. Saurajit's first major leadership post was senior manager for BPA at the Airports Authority of India, where he computerized and/or upgraded accounting and business systems for five international airports. In the United States, he was VP of operations at Software Professionals, Inc., and a principal at the consultancy Pariveda Solutions before joining CG Infinity as president in 2010.

Saurajit is a graduate of the Institute of Chartered Accountants of India. He holds an MBA in information systems from the University of Texas at Arlington and has earned a PMP Certification from the Project Management Institute. His view of the present state of IT and his vision for the future is as follows: "The pandemic taught many businesses that adopting digital channels is no longer optional. The maturity of the cloud has opened up the possibilities of leveraging IT to businesses of all sizes. My teams and I are passionate about helping midsized companies find Blue Oceans by exploiting the powers of the cloud, data, and human capital."

Acknowledgments

This book has two authors who work together in synergy. But the book, like the men's work, also reflects the contributions of many. Each author wishes to thank those who have helped him along the way.

FROM BHOPI DHALL

I was born in a small village in British India near its border with Afghanistan, with my earliest memories being part of a refugee family in Delhi in the 1950s. I remember studying under a kerosene lamp as a child. First and always, I am grateful to the family members who nurtured and supported me through these times. It was then my great fortune to graduate from IIT-Bombay as an electrical engineer.

I feel blessed to have had the opportunity to participate in the computer technology revolution from its beginning, enabled by the development of the transistor. The opportunity arose when I started my professional career as an electrical engineer at Texas Instruments in the late 1960s. TI was the first manufacturer of a germanium transistor. It was the inventor of the silicon transistor and integrated circuits (chips) and became the largest semiconductor company in the world.

One man who helped me to reach this opportunity was Mr. Robert L. Thompson of Kalamazoo, Michigan, who became my godparent in the United States. I met him during my flight to the United States for graduate studies at Michigan Tech. Mr. Thompson was then the president of the Rotary Club of Kalamazoo. He and his wife Elizabeth literally adopted me in the summer of 1968. I lived with them and their three sons during that time, and Mr. Thompson helped me get a very nice summer job, which jump-started my American Dream.

Professionally, I am grateful to TI's senior executive, Mr. Sam K. Smith, for being my mentor throughout my career at the company. In the '60s, under the leadership of Mr. Smith, TI had embarked on developing a supercomputer called the Advanced Scientific Computer for defending against the Soviet Union's nuclear missiles under US Department of Defense sponsorship. Thanks to Sam Smith, I had the privilege of being a member of the design and development team of ASC's processor and memory systems. Today, the whole IT world takes 1s and 0s for granted. My teammates and I had to live through the struggle of making stable and reliable 1s and 0s as we sped up the clock rates. After my departure from TI, Mr. Smith also helped me build my company, CG Infinity.

I am deeply indebted to TI's CEO, Mr. Jerry Jenkins, for trusting me to create and run TI's Digital Light Processing Hardcopy Venture. This gave me great experience in becoming a computer technology entrepreneur, especially under the umbrella of a big, established company.

Beyond TI, I am indebted to Mr. Jon Piasecki, VP of engineering and automotive, and Mr. Peter Dardis, director of engineering, at Branson Ultrasonics Corporation—an industrial automation division of Emerson Electric Company. Mr. Piasecki and Mr. Dardis entrusted me and my startup venture, CG Infinity, with helping Branson engineer their control systems for plastic and metal joining equipment over a period of more than twelve years.

I am also grateful to Mr. Paul Wickberg, president of Verisae, Inc. Mr. Wickberg entrusted me and CG Infinity with helping to develop Verisae's Intelligent Facilities Management System, which was employed by grocery chains in the United States and the United Kingdom. Many more clients have shown similar trust. It has been a pleasure to serve them over the years and to do so along with my brilliant team members at CG Infinity. Together, we have enjoyed the great adventure of bringing out the benefits that digital technology can offer.

On both a personal and professional level, I am indebted to a Silicon Valley pioneer and angel investor, Mr. Kanwal Rekhi. In addition to being my college buddy in Bombay and Michigan, he has been the key investor in CG Infinity, guiding us through all of our business ups and downs for over twenty years.

Finally, and foremost, I am grateful to my wife, Kamla Madan Dhall, who is a barrister at law, London, and earned an LLM from Harvard University. Kamla is admitted to the High Court of London, the Kenya High Court, and the State Bar of Texas. She not only has put up with me for forty-seven years but has also supported me in risking our retirement funds to launch CG Infinity.

FROM SAURAJIT KANUNGO

I owe a great deal to many colleagues and ex-colleagues I have worked with. The same is true of my customer friends across many industries. Ironically, although they pay me to advise them and to implement projects, I am often the one who learns the most from our engagements and interactions.

I have numerous mentors who help me unconditionally. My thanks go to each of them. In the organizations I joined over the last three decades, I have worked under four supervisors and learned much from all of them, especially my coauthor on this book, Bhopi Dhall. He offered me the opportunity to build an awesome company where we continue to grow as people to serve our customers. Last but not least, I am very thankful to my wife, Savita, for her continued support in spite of my idiosyncrasies.